A
LIGHT
in the
MIDST
of
DARKNESS

SUPPORT YOUR LOCAL INDEPENDENT ❶

A LIGHT *in the* MIDST *of* DARKNESS

THE STORY OF A BOOKSHOP, A COMMUNITY AND TRUE LOVE

WALLACE BAINE

Book cover and interior design: Alicia Feltman of Lala Design
Neal Coonerty photo on cover: Shmuel Thaler/*Santa Cruz Sentinel*
Author photo on back cover: Tina Baine
All other photos courtesy of Bookshop Santa Cruz

Printed in the United States of America
FIRST EDITION ISBN 978-0986189852

WELLSTONE CENTER
in the Redwoods

Wellstone Books
an imprint of the Wellstone Center in the Redwoods
858 Amigo Road
Soquel, CA 95073
www.wellstoneredwoods.org

Distributed by Publishers Group West

To my daughters Quinlyn and Casey, and the books
we've shared together

I think that I still have it in my heart someday to paint a book shop with the front yellow and pink, in the evening, and the black passersby — it is such an essentially modern subject. ... I have a great longing to do it like a light in the midst of darkness.

–Vincent Van Gogh,
letter to his brother Theo, November 21, 1889

A town isn't a town without a bookstore. It may call itself a town, but unless it's got a bookstore it knows it's not fooling a soul.

–Neil Gaiman

CONTENTS

CHAPTER 1

A Blood-Mad Enthusiasm

You see tags, dozens, maybe hundreds of them, hanging from the edges of bookshelves like laundry hanging from tenement windows. You're too distracted or preoccupied to notice at first, but each of those tags is a love note. Aimed at you.

This is a place of business, in a downtown district surrounded on all sides by other places of business. It's not the kind of environment where you would expect to encounter a love note. What you're used to are ads, come-ons, appeals from smiling, unthreatening stock-photo models alongside worked-over phrases from copywriters. The tags aren't like that. Each one carries a handwritten message, no more than a couple of sentences, sometimes illustrated like the front of a teenager's notebook, sometimes not. These are not love notes like the ones slipped under the dorm-room door or accompanying a Valentine's Day breakfast in bed. It's likely you wouldn't even know the note writer if he or she were standing right next to you. These are love-triangle notes between the writer, the intended reader – and a book.

We readers live out our lives swinging from one book to the next, and if there's anything we crave as much as time spent with the book we're holding, it's information on where to find the next one. Sure, you have that book-group friend who can't stop talking about Amis and McEwan, your *New York Review of Books*-subscribing sister, that person you know at the gym who's always reading on the treadmill and sharing her opinions whether you want them or not. You're also familiar with the calculations you have to make with those tips, how simpatico they are to your tastes. Sometimes, not very. These tags may represent more misses than hits as well, but they come from book people who share something ineffable with you. Somewhere among them is the portal to your next book, to your next adventure.

These notes are part of the interior design at Bookshop Santa Cruz and other independent bookstores, offered as staff recommendations for browsing shoppers. They have a job to do, to pass on some sort of consumer information to you about the book. When you read them, you see in them, straining through the syntax, pushing against the limits of their inadequate adjectives, a potent, blood-mad enthusiasm that tells you as much about the note's writer at it does about the book they're recommending.

There's the light. There's the love.

My eyes rest on one such note as I scan the fiction section, a testimonial on Richard Adams' *Watership Down*, the world's most famous apocalyptic rabbit novel, a tale of genuine adult-sized dread and broad metaphorical resonance, despite the fact that all its characters are bunnies. I was consumed with this book somewhere around thirteen or fourteen, and the mention of its title still evokes the hot, airless summer evenings I spent with it in the backyard hammock, lost in the intimate act of reading a story that felt like it was written for me alone. Forty years later, I can still access the dark terror that Fiver felt, gripped by a vision that his peaceable rabbit warren was about to be destroyed by some unknown and unstoppable force. I'm flashing on it now as I stand here reading the tag.

Obviously, this Bookshop staffer is as fervent about *Watership Down* as I once was. Her language is spilling from the note. She is not thinking about selling something. She is sharing a piece of herself. "I re-read it every spring without fail," the note says, "and every spring I am again awed by the beauty and complexity of the story and its characters."

Good God, I think, is there a book that I reread every year? Have I allowed literature to seep as deeply into my fatty tissue as this person?

Then, I notice the signature. Will you look at that? The tag was written by someone I know. I have known her since she was a toddler. She was a babysitter for my own daughters, years ago now. I had driven her home several times when she was a teen, maybe with *Watership Down* in her backpack.

Our connection reminds me that I am part of a community, a literary community, centered in this bookshop, in this town. And it is also a confirmation of the energy of great books over time. I had discovered *Watership Down* soon after its publication in the '70s. It was a book of my generation, as much as *The World According to Garp* or *Zen and the Art of Motorcycle Maintenance*. Yet here was another person, decades younger, who had somehow found it as well, offering proof that the book's power hasn't diminished. She and I and every other signature on these many notecards, and probably every idle browser sharing the store with me this moment, are linked in the continuity of literature and love and time.

You know, that just doesn't happen in a hardware store.

We're all accustomed to the idea of a bookstore, which was – and I'm speculating here – invented ten minutes or so after the invention of the book itself. But let's ruminate for a second on just how weird the position of a modern-day bookstore is in Western

3

consumer culture. What other business has to compete with a widespread and, by now, deeply ingrained effort by the government to give away its products for free? Imagine if I proposed a bill in Congress to establish tens of thousands of taxpayer-funded outlets in every town and hamlet in America that would loan out pipe wrenches, post-hole diggers and earth movers to any breathing citizen with a government-issued card. Everybody in Washington, including the statues in the Capitol Rotunda, would laugh such a bill out of town. Yet we tolerate – scratch that, *venerate* – the public library as an absolute public good. Do you know any sane person past the diaper stage who would dare utter the mildest criticism of the public library as a concept? Yeah, me neither.

Bookstores and libraries have existed side by side more or less contentedly for generations and the universe has not yet folded in on itself. The two have even developed a mutually beneficial relationship where each is the other's biggest friend and booster. It's a dogs-marrying-cats situation that we all accept as the natural order. It's as if for books – and books alone – that we are able to live with the most pervasive kind of socialism and the most free-market form of capitalism at the same time.

Why do we draw a big red circle around this specific product for this kind of treatment? The book isn't just one form of media among many others. The book is primal. Each of the world's great religions is centered on a book. The great discoveries and inventions of science are meaningless until translated to a book. As parents, we are uneasy exposing our young children to the still-evolving universe of media formats, but books are as benign as mother's milk, more so to some people.

To readers, books are oxygen, and what's the point of making the case for oxygen? Readers don't need to be told that the stories in books, even ones with pictures, illuminate and invigorate the imagination in a way that movies, video or anything on a screen cannot. We confirm our special love for the book by our behavior. The value of a VHS copy of a movie, even a movie you adore, a movie that changed your life, is close to garbage once you get the DVD, and the DVD is headed for the same fate once you can stream *Eraserhead* (no, seriously, a masterpiece). But tell me with a straight face that you would not go into a burning building to retrieve that copy of *Where the Wild Things Are* that your dad read to you as a kid, or that copy of *The Little Prince* given to you by a friend who is no longer among the living.

If I still have a movie that I've owned for more than ten years, it's only because of laziness and inertia. (Looking for a free copy of *The English Patient*? Come on over! It's yours!) Books, though, that's just a different dimension. If you visit me in my living room or office – don't mind the cat; he just really likes people – I can caress the spines of my books on the shelf and bore you with all kinds of stories.

Really? You don't mind? OK, just one.

This small book here on the top shelf? *The Yosemite* by John Muir? Well, most native-born Californians first experienced Yosemite probably in the back seat of their parents' car, probably distracted by a Game Boy, probably less than enraptured by the majesty of the place and more excited by the French fries at the Ahwahnee. Me, I was lucky. I didn't experience Yosemite until I was in my early twenties when I hiked out from the valley to spend several nights in the backcountry alone. Under any circumstances, it would have been an amazing and deeply moving experience. But this tiny book, a pocket-sized version of Muir's writings about Yosemite, made that experience nothing less than worshipful. Reading Muir aloud, half scared out of my wits by bears, I felt like I was communing not necessarily with nature but with every untamed Scotsman, every adventurous native Miwok, every sentient creature alive or dead equipped with the mind to wonder who had ever gazed upon what I was gazing upon at that moment. That brush with Universal Godhead came from this little book.

People who read do so for a number of complex and interconnected reasons: for escape, for enlightenment, for inspiration, for rapture. Reading allows you to indulge in the quiet of your own interior life without having to answer to the harangues of your inner critic. Reading is solitude with an asterisk. You're alone in all the best senses of being alone, yet you're connected to another mind as well.

Isn't "bookish" just a synonym for "bashful"? Those who love books don't always find a suitable niche in today's Darwinian mercantile society. Entrepreneurial culture favors the networker, the glad-hander. There is no entity that straddles these two worlds more comfortably than the contemporary bookstore. It's one of the few commercial spaces in which we delicate and sensitive book people – to whom the whole messy, materialistic, sharp-elbows world often resembles the floor of the New York Stock Exchange – can feel entirely at home.

Of course, the digital revolution has had roughly the same effect on the book business as that rogue wave had on the *S.S. Poseidon*. Used to be that there was no more complacent business than the downtown bookstore. It was a dark, musty, labyrinthine shop of narrow aisles and imposing bookshelves (on which you might find the occasional napping cat), quiet as a mortuary except for the gentle snoring of the dozing shopkeeper sitting at the front register.

I'm old enough to have experienced these places with their creaking staircases and mildewy air. They seemed indifferent to the prospect of your actually buying something and more concerned that you not loiter. You might even have encountered the occasional, hectoring "This is not a library!" sign. Yet I'm also young enough to prefer what the bookstore has now become – the spacious, well-lit palace of literary pleasure with its couches and cafes, and their sidelines of cards, calendars and posters. It became less like a traditional bookstore and more like a literary theme store in which readers could always find something appealing.

The metamorphosis from the former to the latter was, and continues to be, painful, brought about by big-box discount stores and online retailers (OK, one specific online retailer), and many independent bookstores did not survive it. The sleepy bookstore of yore has largely gone the way of the corner pay phone, not extinct but increasingly rare.

The much publicized shakeout of the bookstore business has forced indie bookstores and those who love them to reassess what the brick-and-mortar bookstore means in the lives of its customers. At one time, that was an absurd question – the bookstore was where you bought books, duh. Today, not only are books easier to obtain than ever, but the ideas and stories contained in them are available in so many different forms and modes of transmission.

That means, nowadays, your indie bookstore has to justify its existence. And for many of them, they have found their raison d'etre in providing exactly that thing that consumerism can provide only in ersatz form: connection, community and, to put a finer point on it, love.

I want to tell you about my favorite bookstore. I want to reflect on its place in my life and the lives of others. Bookshop Santa Cruz is not the biggest, the most well-known or the most visited independent bookstore in the country. It wasn't the first bookstore in town, nor is it the only one today. But it might be the most representative of how such an establishment reflects its community, and even defines it.

When Neal Coonerty, the man who owned and operated Bookshop for most of its fifty-year existence, told me that his customers saved his business, he wasn't speaking metaphorically. Sure, they "saved" it over the years with their dollars when they could have taken their book-buying business elsewhere, but that's not what he's talking about. In 1989, a ruinous earthquake almost destroyed the bookstore. It would have if people who loved the store had not come out of their homes one cloudy fall day with their work boots on and, quite literally, with their muscles and sweat, rescued it. There are beloved institutions all over the world which never get to see that kind of dramatic illustration of what they mean to their communities. Considering the tragic tradeoffs, Coonerty and his staff would probably have rather not seen it either. But they did. And because of it, "love" isn't some frivolous term you apply when you talk about the relationship between this bookstore and this town. It's the very bone and sinew of it.

To claim that Bookshop Santa Cruz will one day celebrate its one hundredth birthday, or that bookstores will be with us always, or that the book itself will live on forever is nothing but an act of faith. It feels good to say it and believe it. Or maybe the opposite is true and all these familiar totems of literature are doomed. I haven't been able to shake Gary Shteyngart's 2010 futuristic comic novel *Super Sad True Love Story*, in which a young person in the uncomfortably near future sees an older guy reading a book on the subway and says, with a grimace of distaste, "Dude, that thing smells like wet socks."

Let's at least celebrate that we don't yet live in Shteyngart's world, that there are still enough of us that like the smell of wet socks.

Love it, even.

CHAPTER 2

The View From Santa Cruz

Tucked in along the southern frontier of the San Francisco Bay Area, Santa Cruz, California, is a surf town. Famously name-checked in the Beach Boys' "Surfin' USA," it has for decades been a destination, and often home, for many of the West Coast's finest professional surfers, and several thousand more amateurs to boot. For almost as long, it has been engaged in a not always light-hearted rivalry with Huntington Beach in Southern California for the title "Surf City." (If we're going to litigate the matter, Huntington Beach is nowhere to be found in "Surfin' USA," even though the song's writer, Brian Wilson, lived a lot of closer to Huntington than he did to Santa Cruz. So what does that tell you?)

That Santa Cruz is also a book town does not seem the least bit incongruous to anyone who lives there. Despite the persistent stereotypes of both surfers and readers, there is significant overlap between the two, and that's nowhere more prevalent than in Santa Cruz. (Do surfers in the queue for the next wave at Steamer Lane kill time parsing Munro and Eggers? Not likely, but certainly not unthinkable.)

There is ample evidence to suggest that the laid-back vibe of Santa Cruz has been just as appealing to writers as it has been to surfers. The literary equivalent to Santa Cruz's shout-out in "Surfin' USA" (though not nearly as danceable) may be the town's prominent role in Wallace Stegner's majestic 1971 novel *Angle of Repose*, which provides a vivid portrait of the area in the late nineteenth century and places it in the context of the wild and rootless American West. Stegner's son and daughter-in-law, both writers, lived in Santa Cruz for years, as did one of his most well-known literary disciples, James D. Houston, a Mount Rushmore figure in Santa Cruz's literary history. Houston's lyrical and wistful 1964 essay "The View from Santa Cruz" captured the character of the place before its peace-and-love cultural makeover. It had the audacity to plumb the depths of the California romantic myth and return to the surface with something worth keeping. Houston was, at least in the eyes of one worshipful and unworthy would-be writer, California personified.

Poets, a class of folks justly celebrated for their sensitivity to their surroundings, are rife in Santa Cruz. If there were any kind of economy for poetry, it might be to Santa Cruz what oil is for Midland, Texas. The area has nursed a healthy poetry scene, including public readings, festivals and publications, for at least forty years. I know a guy who writes poetry on a typewriter for passersby on the sidewalks of downtown, another one who sold (or, attempted to sell) his self-published chapbooks on the street every day for twenty years. A well-known widely published local poet has erected a plexiglass box outside her home that she stocks with poems every day, free for the taking. I've seen open-mic poetry readings in clubs, libraries, even laundromats. Adrienne Rich, the kind of poet they teach in comp-lit classes, lived the second half of her life in Santa Cruz.

For whatever reason – my money's on the aroma of the bay laurel tree on hot afternoons in late summer, or maybe the relaxed attitude toward weed – the Santa Cruz area has been a magnet for contemplative and creative types for much of its history. I first came to Santa Cruz shortly after the devastating Loma Prieta earthquake as a young reporter assigned to cover the cultural beat for the daily newspaper and I have never stopped being amazed at the sheer output of the locals, many of them originally from some other place, in all of the arts: literature, music, dance, theater, the visual arts, soap bubble performance art (yep), Daliesque accordion playing (not making that up either), you name it. I think the cliché "like drinking from a fire hydrant" must have been first uttered by a cultural reporter in Santa Cruz.

Within my first year on the arts beat, I profiled a performance artist – think Wednesday Addams growing up into a proto-Lady GaGa with literary aspirations – that ran with the bold headline: "Dominatrix, Stripper, Satanist, Poet." Nobody in Santa Cruz blinked an eye, just another self-actualizing neighbor. Somewhere around that time, I also interviewed a prominent playwright/film director who told me, with a straight face, that there's a potent creative force (gas? radiation waves? ghostly spirits from beyond?) seeping out from the nearby San Andreas Fault that is the source of his creative energy and that of every artist within thirty miles of the fault line. Yanking my chain? Maybe. Still, the sheer volume of creatives in the area begs for an explanation. That's as good as any other, I suppose.

Maybe the best way to understand Santa Cruz is through the prism of rose-colored glasses, or whatever color was popular back in the 1960s. Santa Cruz's cultural identity is still very much attuned to the '60s. It is no happenstance that the local university today houses the Grateful Dead's official archives, or that a wide variety of Dead tribute bands, local and otherwise, perform regularly in area clubs. For much of the 2000s, the most popular local band was a group that performed the Beatles' *White Album* song by song to sold-out audiences. It's not true that "Santa Cruz" is Spanish for "Pink Floyd," but it might as well be.

Not that Santa Cruz today is any kind of '60s theme park, any more than the Haight in San Francisco is. Peace signs, casual nudity and flowers in the hair are rare, but not unheard of. You can, in fact, buy tie-dye from a guy sitting on the sidewalk. Second-hand shops and coffeehouses are plentiful. You can find a hacky sack when you need one. The term "man" is a common form of punctuation in local speech. "Dude" is not used exclusively in reference to dudes. The person in the downtown information kiosk sports a magenta-colored thatch of hair shooting up from her forehead like some Hawaiian water bird.

This is the environment in which Bookshop Santa Cruz has evolved and which it today reflects. It is a place that has embraced its image as the town's cultural living room, even though sometimes it must have felt like a bedroom. (In its early days, one of Bookshop's most eccentric features was a king-size water bed that customers were free to use for, well, use your imagination.)

Bookshop itself is a creature of the '60s, opening in 1966. Yes, Santa Cruz has a history of bohemianism that dates back long before the hippie era. It was even home to a small avant-garde of musicians and other freethinkers who gathered at the subversive coffeehouse the Sticky Wicket to listen to subversive folk music and tug meaningfully at their goatees. They were led by the brilliant composer (and John Cage protégé) Lou Harrison, who established a bleeding-edge musical festival that still exists today. Also, let's not forget that surf culture, abloom in Santa Cruz long before the Gidget-fueled surf craze of the '60s, cultivated a certain inherently rebellious subculture. Many of the younger surfers in town served as the pioneers of the hippie movement.

Still, before the mid-1960s, Santa Cruz was mostly known as a conservative, square-shouldered, *American Graffiti* kind of town that attracted summer tourists to its colorful oceanfront boardwalk and beckoned retirees with affordable homes in quiet neighborhoods cooled by morning fogs and sea breezes. It is here we must go to get to the beginning of the Bookshop Santa Cruz story, before the University of California came to town and changed everything, before Bookshop itself was even a thing. Like most stories rooted in the '60s, it begins with the Beatles. It begins with the sound of one kind of love, and the image of a very different kind of love.

Stand here beside me on Pacific Avenue, in front of the grand old St. George Hotel. It is late summer 1964 and we are here to witness the grand opening of the Hip Pocket bookstore. Look around, and you'll see the curious downtowners. Mostly, we're talking Suits and Dresses, hairdos and black-framed glasses. They're here to welcome the newcomer to the downtown scene. There's also something else, a crowd of more loose-limbed folks dressed like gypsies and vagabonds. Who are these people? And where did they come from? The Suits and Dresses seem baffled.

The two partners in the Hip Pocket are out-of-towners, strangers to the close-knit Santa Cruz business community, and, frankly, they seem to be a couple of odd ducks. They've rigged up a sound system, a hi-fi as the kids call it, that blasts music out into the streets. You and I, we know the tune immediately. It's the Beatles' irresistibly jangly "I Want to Hold Your Hand," which was a huge hit on the radio just a few months before. The Suits and Dresses, some of them just grin, desperate to appear agreeable. Others look at each other in befuddlement.

Look there, above the bookstore's entrance. There is something hidden under a drape-like covering, something set to be unveiled. One of the new store's owners gestures to the mayor, who steps forward for the unveiling. He tugs at the rope hanging from the covering and it falls to the ground.

Maybe if the music weren't so loud, we'd be able to hear the gasps and the murmurs. We can certainly see the faces, frowning, slack-jawed, gazing up in the direction of the hotel's second floor. Maybe, despite the music, we can hear the "Oh, my God" gasps peppered in among the laughter and the applause. We can certainly see some residents of the old St. George, leaning out their windows, gaping and pointing.

And there it is: A larger than life copper sculpture of two figures, a man and woman – a nude man and woman, standing together, gazing into each other's faces, reaching their hands down in an only partially successful effort to cover their nethers. What we have here is a case of private parts going public, about as public as you can get. Sure, the female figure might make some people uncomfortable, but there's nothing too explicit in it. No, it's the male figure that's attracting the stares. Congratulations, you have just been introduced to the most infamous piece of copper tubing in this town's history.

And that, boys and girls, is how Santa Cruz's signature bookstore was born. For the record, the Hip Pocket was an entirely different enterprise than Bookshop Santa Cruz, but it opened in the very spot where Bookshop is today. It blazed the trail that Bookshop would follow. Yes, you could buy a book in town before 1964; the Sunnyside Bookshop, for example, catered to local artists and book lovers as far back as the Great Depression. The downtown store displayed local art on the walls and hosted a series of literary lectures on everything from Emily Dickinson to the art and craft of bookbinding. Still, the aspirations at Hip Pocket were in tune to the groovy vibe of the Beat Generation, in sync with City Lights in San Francisco or Cody's Books in Berkeley.

The store's partners, Peter Demma and Ron Bevirt, were intent on opening a bookstore somewhere in Northern California. A couple of years earlier, the two men flashed on Santa Cruz while sitting in the mineral hot springs at Big Sur, more than an hour's drive to the south. The University of California had announced that it would open a new school in Santa Cruz, and Demma and Bevirt were among the first to anticipate how a university might transform the beach town.

The Hip Pocket was open for less than two years, but in that short time achieved its own literary legacy. It found its way into Tom Wolfe's *The Electric Kool-Aid Acid Test*, a landmark of the new journalism of the 1960s. In fact, the first "acid test" happened next door to Santa Cruz in the small community of Soquel. Ken Kesey and Allen Ginsberg visited, and it became a favorite haunt of perhaps the most well-known literary muse in postwar American literature, Jack Kerouac's pal and a notorious figure of the Beat Generation, Neal Cassady.

James D. Houston, who settled in Santa Cruz with his wife Jeanne in 1962, remembers that Cassady visited the Hip Pocket on the day it opened. Cassady was the driver of the infamous school bus, nicknamed "Further," that was painted in a galactic supernova of color, carrying Kesey and his lunatic fringe of friends and cronies known as the Merry Pranksters (the unofficial membership of which included both of Hip Pocket's owners). Just before the unveiling of the nudes over the store's entrance, the old bus came ambling down Pacific Avenue, recalls Houston, with Kesey sitting on its roof, documenting his own arrival with a hand-held movie camera. In a 1989 essay, Houston writes, "The street has somehow filled with gypsy girls and VW vans and bearded men in sheepskin jackets."

Cassady, the prime inspiration behind Kerouac's immortal novel *On the Road*, found Santa Cruz a comfortable way station in his later years. He was, as his literary reputation confirms, a man always on the move, but his wife and children lived in nearby Los Gatos, and he often found himself in Santa Cruz. And when he was in town, Cassady was often hanging around at the Hip Pocket. His son and daughter both remember seeing him there, more often than not entertaining an audience with discourses on life, literature and philosophy, more often than not strung out on speed. He could also be found occasionally working the cash register at the Hip.

Neal Cassady's public image is entirely a creation of literature. Few, even in his day, would have recognized a photo of the man. We know him from the pages of *On the Road* as the restless spirit Dean Moriarty, the impulsive and depraved hedonist, the spiritual daredevil, the eternal child in constant search for the perpetual now. Maybe he was, in 1964, already something of a relic of a passing era. Maybe he sensed that the world was about to roll over on him. Of the Beat icons, only Ginsberg successfully made the transition to the Age of Aquarius. Kerouac's last great book – *Big Sur,* inspired by the bohemian enclave on the precipice of California's most spectacular piece of coastline – had already been written, and no doubt featured prominently at the Hip Pocket. The TV series *Route 66,* popular at the time, had trapped the wild aimlessness and discontent of *On the Road* and tamed it, turning out a sanitized version of it to Americans on their suburban sofas. By the end of the decade, Kerouac and Cassady would both be dead.

The Hip Pocket sat on the cusp between eras, between the pushback against the mass conformity of the Eisenhower years and the flowering of what was at that point just starting to bud. The store's reaction was to become notorious, provocative, fearlessly, maybe even recklessly, devoted to art and free expression. The copper nudes that hovered over the Hip's front entrance were the work of Ron Boise, a Bay Area artist who had also done a series of sculptures he called *Kama Sutra* in which he rendered sheet metal taken from wrecked cars into sexually explicit poses. During the same year that the Hip Pocket opened, *Kama Sutra* was setting tongues wagging in San Francisco in a gallery adjacent to City Lights bookstore. The Boise nudes at the Hip were not just "shock the squares" agitprop. They represented a continuity with the robust scene in San Francisco. It was just in time for the next cultural ground shift.

The year after the Hip Pocket opened (and the year before it closed down), the University of California christened a new campus in Santa Cruz. The arrival of the new UC, established on picturesque ranch lands just north of town, coincided with the dawn of the '60s. It legitimized a cultural swing toward a more bohemian vibe. What's more, the new university was established on an avant-garde educational model – no letter grades! – and, as a result, it attracted a more adventurous and open-minded kind of student.

That fall of '65, downtown merchants watched warily from their storefronts as buses disgorged the first class of students from the new campus. To the shopkeepers and business owners, the kids looked clean-cut and well-behaved in those early days. But in a matter of weeks, the hair began to get longer as the skirts got shorter. The monochromatic town was going Day-Glo, and the Hip Pocket was the most high-profile symbol of that gradual transformation.

Demma and Bivert never seemed very interested in fitting in with their fellow downtown merchants. Worse, from the viewpoint of the defenders of community decency, the bookstore sold nudist magazines and other "smut." Longtime Merry Prankster Lee Quarnstrom, a Hip Pocket employee, recalls that the bookstore was "hassled quite a bit" by the police, the fire department, truant officers looking for kids skipping school. A local minister initiated a campaign against the store. "One night I remember hearing him on the radio," says Quarnstrom. "He said, 'There's a sewer running through the main street of Santa Cruz and it's called the Hip Pocket bookstore.'"

Finally, owners Demma and Bevirt got into serious hot water when the local district attorney's office decided to prosecute them for displaying "obscene" photos on the wall of the store that showed full frontals of naked men. The photos were from well-known photographer Walter Chappell and were anthropological in nature, a distinction apparently lost on the D.A.'s office. The obscenity case was thrown out, but that didn't make Demma and

Bevirt (known among the Merry Pranksters by his nickname "Hassler") any better as businessmen. Marketing was still something of a dark art for the two, and they made no effort to stock the store with bestsellers. Instead they sold art books, obscure philosophy books, Greek literature. We can't confirm it, but it's a safe bet that the guys behind the Hip Pocket were never accused of being commercially savvy. At one point a sheriff's deputy took over the register, rang up a customer for a $1.95 paperback and stuffed the money into his satchel to take to the store's creditors.

"I don't think they thought of it so much as 'We're going to go down and take this little town by the throat and shake it until it becomes Greenwich Village west,'" Quarnstrom remembers. "They just thought, 'You can't buy any good books in Santa Cruz, so let's open a bookstore.'"

If the Hip Pocket was doomed, it was certainly not a reflection of Santa Cruz's growing counterculture. The new university was bringing in fresh blood for the hippie revolution every year and if the Hip Pocket was not going to be there to cater to them, something else would. That "something else" would turn out to be Bookshop Santa Cruz, which opened in November 1966. The new bookseller in town was Ron Lau, a former publisher's agent who was much smarter about how to maintain a business than his Merry Prankster predecessors. He and his wife, Sharon, were no squares.

"He was a unique character," is how Bookshop's first employee, Jon Scoville, remembers Ron. "He was a salesman type, but he loved to read. He loved ideas and political issues. He slept up in the attic of the bookstore, dropped acid a couple of times, just to find out what it was all about." True, they weren't going to have Neal Cassady at the register or giant copper nudes welcoming shoppers every morning. Yet they knew enough to maintain a symbiotic relationship with a new coffeehouse next door called the Catalyst, they were eager to cater to students, and they knew how to keep the doors open. A new era had begun.

CHAPTER 3

The Electricity
of Social Change

Here's something to throw out on the table in your next bar-room argument, if you happen to be in a bar with a bunch of music snobs, comic-book nerds and newspaper critics: What was the greatest year in the history of American popular culture? As they say in group therapy, there are no wrong answers. (Scratch that: there are a *few* wrong answers.) A vast majority would probably choose a year somewhere in their teenage-dom; I carry a torch for '77 myself. But if you crunch the data and look at it dispassionately, 1966 is an undeniably strong candidate. There's a metaphor that backs up the '66 argument that I keep coming back to: For the first time ever, one of the three major television networks (NBC) began broadcasting all its programs in color. Yep, 1966 was literally the year the cultural world shook off black-and-white and went full color.

In keeping with that colorful transformation, '66 also spawned a number of what we consider pop-culture holy relics today: The Beach Boys' *Pet Sounds*, the Beatles' *Revolver* and Bob Dylan's *Blonde on Blonde*. *Star Trek* was born that year. Ditto *The Endless Summer*, *Twister*, the Monkees, *Batman* (Adam West version), the Black Panthers, TV's *How the Grinch Stole Christmas*, Jefferson Airplane and, perhaps most significantly of all, the miniskirt. The Doors, Jimi Hendrix and the Grateful Dead all signed their first contracts. Hunter S. Thompson published his first book (*Hell's Angels*) and Truman Capote his greatest (*In Cold Blood*). Raquel Welch, Woody Allen and full-frontal nudity made their movie debuts. Sandy Koufax threw his last pitch in the big leagues and Nolan Ryan his first. Walt Disney died and J.J. Abrams was born.

And Bookshop Santa Cruz opened its doors for the first time on November 7, 1966, the day before Ronald Reagan was elected as governor of California. The store was opened and run for seven years by former publishing sales agent Ron Lau and his wife, Sharon. Unlike Peter Demma and Ron Bivert at the Hip Pocket, the Laus knew something about the publishing business and had connections there.

Bookshop's founding is intertwined with the establishment of another business, every bit as famous locally as Bookshop itself. For several decades now, the Catalyst has been Santa Cruz's premier night club and live music showcase. In its early days, however, the Catalyst was something altogether different. Opening in the same year as Bookshop, it was a coffeehouse, a deli, a bar and a casual meet-up spot that occupied the ground floor of the old St. George Hotel. True to its name, the Catalyst created a downtown hangout for all the bohos and weirdos that were first attracted by the Hip Pocket. Together, the two businesses represented a vaguely transgressive place where UC students (and faculty) could congregate.

A small corridor connected the Catalyst and Bookshop, and that passageway was central to the symbiotic relationship between the two businesses (though it was also safe passage for a lot of stolen books). Together Bookshop and the Catalyst formed a cultural nexus for the Now Generation (as the Boomers used to call themselves, unironically), a place to Be Here Now and argue about Dylan going electric over twenty-five-cent coffee. Yet that symbiosis didn't happen by accident.

A man by the name of Byron Stookey, a Harvard-educated administrator who was instrumental in the creation of UC Santa Cruz, watched the Hip Pocket go down in flames. He must have figured that after starting a university from scratch the year before, it would be a cinch to create an off-campus culture in conservative Santa Cruz. He helped Ron and Sharon Lau get Bookshop up and running, and formed a co-op to open the Catalyst. By the end of the year, students, professors, street poets, bohos, literary types, loiterers, artists, hippies and other curiosities were flocking to the Catalyst and Bookshop, ideally to grab a copy of *Valley of the Dolls* at Bookshop and search out the dirty parts over coffee and brownies at the Cat.

Ron and Sharon Lau knew next to nothing about Santa Cruz before opening Bookshop. Sharon, still in her early twenties, had worked at the legendary Tro Harper Books in San Francisco, and she was more than a little alarmed to see empty storefronts when she first came to downtown Santa Cruz. She remembers driving up the recently completed Highway 1 freeway to work, marveling at the lack of traffic, wondering to herself, "Did they build this just for us?"

Those of Sharon Lau's generation, the early Boomers, got to witness the blossoming of a counterculture that was sudden and irreversible, if not in their own hometowns, then certainly in the mass media. Yes, there had always been some kind of artistic or sexual avant-garde throughout the twentieth century. But the amplifying effects of television and mass culture, controlled by marketing minds eager to sell to a massive, emerging demographic of young people, brought on all kinds of new social freedoms. The electricity of social change was especially jolting in Santa Cruz, thanks to the opening of the UC campus, which initiated Santa Cruz's rapid evolution into Berkeley-by-the-Beach. And the laboratory where that evolution was happening was at the Catalyst and Bookshop Santa Cruz.

Ron Lau and Jon Scoville were still building and stocking shelves the morning the store first opened its doors. Sharon was giving birth in San Francisco to the couple's first child. There was no ribbon-cutting or nude statue unveiling, but UC's Byron Stookey was there all day. Scoville remembers the store did just under $100 in sales and that everybody was ecstatic.

When Bookshop first opened for business, its staff was dressed in conservative suits and ties, but almost immediately that look was abandoned. (Throughout his run as the Bookshop's owner, Ron Lau was famous for wearing shorts and sandals every day, no matter the season or the weather.) With the clientele from the next-door Catalyst streaming through the Portal of Stolen Books and curious faculty and students peeking in, Bookshop began to take on a personality. Its inventory began to reflect the interests of the era.

The store tried to be as broad as possible in its selection, with a variety of cheap paperbacks and bestsellers, for example, and catered to students with textbook sales. At the same time, there was an opportunity to shape the store's inventory to match the expanding curiosities of Northern California's readers. In those early years, publishers were putting out a lot of titles in response to a growing interest in subjects such as Eastern mysticism and spirituality, psychedelia and alternative lifestyles, and Santa Cruz was gobbling them up. The year Bookshop opened, the British philosopher Alan Watts published his *The Book: On the Taboo Against Knowing Who You Are*. The next year, the San Francisco novelist Richard Brautigan put out his most famous work, *Trout Fishing in America,* followed in short order by the apocalyptic *In Watermelon*

Sugar. A mysterious, anonymously authored two-thousand-page book on the nature of God, *The Urantia Book*, sold nicely, as did the poetry of William Blake. The title of Abbie Hoffman's *Steal This Book* was often taken literally. *The Autobiography of a Yogi*, Ram Dass' guide to living *Be Here Now*, the far-seeing *Future Shock* by Alvin Toffler, Marshall McLuhan's *The Medium is the Massage*, Alex Comfort's *The Joy of Sex*, the groundbreaking self-knowledge book *Gestalt Therapy Verbatim* by Esalen icon Fritz Perls, all these books formed the foundation of a distinctly California-flavored intellectual refocusing, and none of them were easy to find in mainstream bookstores.

Ron Lau particularly liked the works of Carlos Castaneda, a Peruvian-born American anthropologist, whose books documented his work as an apprentice to a Yaqui Indian shaman. Coupled with Dee Brown's searing *Bury My Heart at Wounded Knee*, Castaneda's books fed an exploding interest among white middle-class readers in Native American spirituality and history. Also popular at Bookshop throughout the late 1960s and early '70s was a publishing phenomenon known as *The Whole Earth Catalog,* by the quintessential San Francisco idealist Stewart Brand. It was a large-format quasi-periodical on newsprint that was brimming with references, reviews, essays and ideas on a wide range of topics from self-sufficient living to alternative energy to engineering, all behind a cover illustrated with a photo of Earth from space, an image still novel enough that it was capable of blowing many minds, dope-enhanced or not. The *WEC* was republished frequently to keep the information as fresh as possible. Several decades later, Apple superhero Steve Jobs likened the book to the next best thing to Google, before the internet.

In 1969, downtown Santa Cruz underwent a radical facelift as conventional Pacific Avenue transformed into the Pacific Garden Mall, a leafy, Edenic, eccentrically designed pedestrian oasis in which the street snaked through the commercial district, mimicking a river. The same year, Bookshop Santa Cruz moved to a new site across the street and up the block. Ron Lau got an opportunity to buy a building, what was once a grocery store, and he jumped at the chance. The move severed the unique relationship that Bookshop had with the Catalyst. Like many other countercultural phenomena of the 1960s, the heady vibe of bohemian idealism was morphing into something else entirely by the end of the decade and, within a few years, the Catalyst was sold and also moved to a new location, shedding its hippie coffeehouse spirit to become a conventional, albeit successful, nightclub and concert venue.

The move gave the Laus room to expand the bookstore. The new space was much larger on its ground floor, and it also had a basement to which Bookshop eventually moved its textbook sales. More space meant more literary offerings and the store began to sell some of the pioneering titles in what are today thriving subgenres in the publishing world: fitness, self-help, computers/software. Mainstream books still paid the freight, but feminist polemics, new age spirituality guides and socio-political journalism were also prominently featured, selling right alongside such mystifying bestsellers of the era as *Jonathan Livingston Seagull* (millennials, ask your parents).

Also popular, the waterbed. As if to show off its bigger space, Ron Lau set up a king-sized waterbed smack in the middle of the bookstore's main floor. From the mid-'70s into the '80s, waterbeds represented a booming lifestyle fad, a perfect swingin' singles accessory for the corduroy-wearing, mustache-sporting, *Playboy*-reading hipster of the time. (The waterbed didn't even exist before 1968, when a San Francisco design student reimagined a new version of an older design of a waterbed that was used for therapeutic reasons in the 1800s. Bookshop Santa Cruz was an early adopter.)

The waterbed was not just for looks. Shoppers were welcome to lounge around on it as they contemplated a book or two. It sent the same signal that overstuffed chairs send to customers today, though with slightly more suggestive connotations: Relax, take it easy, love the one you're with, keep on truckin', what's your hurry?

Poet and author Patrice Vecchione grew up in Santa Cruz and as a young teen, she remembers meeting her friends after school at the bookshop, where four or five of them would climb onto the waterbed together. "We would find this book of artistic photographs of naked female torsos and my girlfriends and I would sit on the waterbed looking at these risqué photos, wondering what our breasts would look like." Sharon Lau told me that the waterbed was always the center of attention in the store and that occasionally she would find someone sleeping on it. "Unless they were causing trouble, we saw no reason to move them," she laughs.

Also adding to the bookstore's personality was the resident cat. Steve Jensen, who ran the Bookshop textbook department in the '70s, remembers a gray female, named Marilyn because she tended to lounge on the bookshelves in much the same pose as Marilyn Monroe in her famous *Playboy* nude shoot. The cat that most remember from the old days was Walter, named for Walt Whitman, an orange-ish male. He was, in fact, the first of several Walters, the name handed down through generations of Bookshop cats, a la "Lassie."

By the early '70s, the candy-colored dream of the hippie era was beginning to sour and occasionally the magic bus veered toward the moral abyss, especially in California where the Charles Manson murders ushered in an era of madness. Whether or not you're inclined to link them to the '60s counterculture and its celebration of drug use, or merely media sensationalism, lurid and horrifying crimes became a national obsession. Santa Cruz was in the middle of it all. Between 1970 and 1973, Santa Cruz was terrorized by the crimes of three separate serial killers and, for a while, the names of Frazier, Kemper and

Mullin were as well known locally as Crosby, Stills and Nash. For a short time, the city had to endure the kind of tagline that haunts the nightmares of municipal politicians everywhere: "The Murder Capital of the World." It was a title that was revived ten years later in the teen vampire film *The Lost Boys*, still probably the most famous film to have been shot in Santa Cruz. Mercifully, for the tourism bureau and Santa Cruz boosters everywhere, *The Lost Boys* changed the name of Santa Cruz to Santa Carla.

Through it all, Bookshop functioned as a sanctuary from the insanity of murder, war and political unrest and a prism through which to make sense of it. Though the bookstore carried such titles as *Helter Skelter*, Vincent Bugliosi's bestselling account of the Manson story, it was still a shelter from the storm for book lovers. As a girl, Patrice Vecchione fell hard for an anthology of poetry called *Reflections on a Gift of Watermelon Pickle*. She saw the book on the shelves at Bookshop Santa Cruz, lamenting that she didn't have enough money to buy it. She took it down and hid it in the economics section of the store until her babysitting fund grew enough for her to afford it. "It tells you something," she says, "that the book was still there months later when I finally was able to buy it."

In early 1973, Ron Lau received a phone call. It was from a guy named Neal Coonerty. Coonerty had heard a rumor that Bookshop Santa Cruz was for sale. Lau said thanks but no thanks, it's not for sale. A couple of weeks later, Lau called Coonerty back. Maybe he would consider selling the bookstore after all, he said. Let's talk.

CHAPTER 4

The Beating Heart

I can't count how many times I've wandered into Bookshop Santa Cruz, either with a specific goal in mind, or just as a result of the inertia or aimless drift of a free hour. Whoever first called this bookstore "Santa Cruz's living room" must have done so because you'll often find yourself, as if in your own living room, standing there slack-jawed wondering "What did I come in here for?" In middle age, I've found that I'm visiting more often, mainly because the appeal of pizza, T-shirts and the other blandishments of competing downtown retailers has diminished to a vanishing point of irrelevance. Books, though, continue to exert a gravitational pull.

Frankly, it's something of a miracle that I ever come to this bookstore at all, seeing as how it was the scene of one of the more acute (but ultimately harmless) public humiliations of my life. In 2010, I was invited to Bookshop to promote a newly published collection of my Sunday humor columns for the daily paper. It was a most gratifying invitation to my writerly ego, but horrifying to the quivering jellyfish of anxiety that controls my every waking thought. For my entire life, I've been subject to a mild stutter. (I only say "mild" because I've met people who've shown me what severe stuttering is; but when I was a kid, my stuttering felt like the afflictions of Job.)There's a reason I grew up to be a writer: to avoid public speaking, or any kind of speaking.

On the evening of the book signing I was floored to find the place packed. People were standing in the aisles, leaning on pillars, struggling to find a line of sight. I spied people in the crowd I hadn't seen in years, friends whom I knew lived a long distance away, well-known faces I would have bet a week's salary had no idea who I was. I'm sure I looked like a Christian about to be tossed to the lions. What agony awaits me tonight? What would be the cost to my reputation and self-image if I just bolted toward the exit and continued running down the street like Forrest Gump?

I was genuinely surprised by what happened next, and to this day, I'm surprised that I was surprised. Just a few minutes into my reading, despite the fact that my stutter had not come out of its cave, my sweat glands began to dramatically malfunction, mostly in a broad band across my forehead. First, I ignored it, frightened to draw any focus away from the delivery of what I was reading. Then, I deftly reached up and flicked a thumb across my brow. My reading glasses began to slide down my nose. I needed a napkin, then a bandanna, then a beach towel, then, perhaps, a paramedic. I had nothing. I looked up at the crowd, only to see them through a scrim, like a window in the rain. Wait, were my eyeballs sweating too?

Suddenly, the bookstore felt like hell's boiler room. A fat plop of moisture hit the page from which I was reading. My wife quietly stepped up and placed a paper towel on the lectern. I read with a fury of self-loathing in defiance of whatever tone that the prose called for. I prayed earnestly for a near-fatal stroke. Then I prayed for a fatal one. What followed was worse: I survived, only to sit at a table as every meaningful person in my life one by one approached with a look of pity and some meant-to-be-comforting remarks that told me only that no one had heard a word I said and that I looked like I had been trapped in a Swedish sauna for three hours. The people at Bookshop did not pass along the carpet-cleaning bill after I had lost a third of my body weight in their store. That speaks to their common decency.

At my next reading, at the Capitola Book Café, I arrived prepared, with a belly full of a beta-blockers and sporting a bright orange headband à la Bjorn Borg. The sweating was only slightly less catastrophic. Toward the end of the ordeal, a friend informed me that what had just happened to me was exactly the reason that David Foster Wallace (with whom I felt an incidental kinship because we shared a name and a birth year) always wore a bandanna. I laughed for the first time all night. That's the kind of thing you'd only hear in a bookstore.

Over the years, it's safe to say that I've had transcendent experiences within the walls of Bookshop Santa Cruz. Most were private – in the pre-internet days, as a young reporter, I would park my keister in one of Bookshop's comfy chairs, while on the clock, and read for hours about California history in the name of "research." Others were quite public, like the in-store interview I conducted with the great journalist Barbara Ehrenreich about the nature of consciousness and a mystical experience she had when she was seventeen. Ehrenreich has spent much of her formidable career as a prominent and outspoken atheist, and here she was with me in front of about a hundred onlookers, talking for the first time about a "dissociative" episode she had that was terrifying and confusing. "The world flamed into life," she described it. "There were no visions, no prophetic voices, no visits by totemic animals, just this blazing everywhere." After that night, my vision of what happens inside a bookstore expanded a bit. I no longer reflexively roll my eyes when I hear it referred to as a "temple." A bookstore is not a church. But it is one of the few public places where talking about the limits of human experience and what lies beyond the material world doesn't seem bizarre and incongruous. You want pizza, go across the street. You want a potentially life-changing idea? This must be the place.

Do bookstores create writers? Well, sure. How can anyone deny such a thing? But many things create writers. Boredom creates writers. So do loneliness, shyness, rage, trauma, thwarted love, bad parentage, ugly breakups and (perhaps at the top of the list) the generalized existentialist stress inherent in figuring out the puzzle of how to be human. Bookstores certainly create readers, and writers inevitably arise from the ranks of readers. And, among readers, bookstores create a sense of literary anticipation. It takes a reader to see the possibilities of exciting new worlds latent in a shelf of books.

I grew up in suburbia, in a house constructed with built-in bookshelves that compelled my parents, who were not avid readers, to find books just for the sake of competent interior decorating. Which is why we had two sets of encyclopedias, the World Book and something called Funk & Wagnalls. (The mystifying practice of buying books just for looks continues today and contributes to a healthy industry of selling books by the foot, for that homeowner who just has to have a wall of only yellow-spined books to match the sofa.) My only viable bookstore option was the B. Dalton's in the mall whose selection was only marginally more interesting than my parent's incoherent mishmash of encyclopedias, Dale Carnegie titles and Michener imitators back home. I didn't fall down the rabbit hole of bookstore loitering until college.

As it turns out, a bookstore was at the center of Santa Cruz novelist Jonathan Franzen's interior life growing up. Franzen, who has attained the kind of prominence that used to be more common in a pre-television, pre-internet age when novelists were often considered cultural superstars, told me about the beloved bookstore of his youth, the Webster Groves Bookshop on the outskirts of St. Louis. It was a small place, about six hundred square feet. Young Jonathan grew up in a budget-minded middle-class family and, as a result, he did most of his book acquisition at the public library, so the bookstore was an aspirational place for him. "I'd get books as presents in high school," he says. "And they would come with the Webster's Bookshop seal. When I would open them, they would all have that crisp, Webster's brand-new book smell." (Webster Groves Bookshop closed its doors after fifty years in the summer of 2016.)

Franzen didn't much connect to bookstores again until he discovered Bookshop Santa Cruz shortly before the publication of his breakout 2001 book *The Corrections*. Since then, he has opened the tours of his landmark novels *Freedom* and *Purity* at events hosted by Bookshop. Franzen's novels rank among the most robust and relevant of the new millennium, which has made him one of the few literary novelists to achieve widespread mainstream fame. His eyeglasses have even made him iconic, which is why he often draws double takes when spotted on one of his regular shopping visits to Bookshop.

"It's the only place I buy books now," he says. "It's as easy to order a book that is not in stock at Bookshop as it is with Amazon. I'm hostile to Amazon. It's an evil monopoly and should not be trusted or patronized."

Franzen also stresses the importance of the role of Bookshop and similar bookstores in maintaining the careers of a broader range of writers in the literary world. "To the extent that there is a literary culture in this country, it needs the stars, but it also needs the people who are really good but have a somewhat narrower national audience. Those authors remain commercially viable because of the independents. They actually have a chance to sell thirty thousand copies and live." His connection to Bookshop now, he says, has a lot to do with people. "It seems nearly half my friends in Santa Cruz either now work for Bookshop or have in the past worked for Bookshop."

Santa Cruz author Laurie R. King has a relationship to Bookshop that goes back decades to when she was a student of religion at UC Santa Cruz. She's the widow of the late Noel King, a brilliant and probing mind on the subject of spirituality and a longtime faculty member at UC Santa Cruz (who could have played the lead role in the Rip Van Winkle biopic). Noel once kept me enthralled for close to three hours at his country home, chatting about the irreducible truths that connect all religious traditions. Laurie is also possessed of an irrepressible intellectual curiosity and she has become a publishing phenomenon for slyly folding in richly realized historical worlds in her mystery novels. She is best known for her popular series of mysteries featuring her heroine Mary Russell, the plucky and much-younger wife of Sherlock Holmes. She also wrote an essay on Bookshop in the collection My Bookstore: Writers Celebrate Their Favorite Places to Browse, Read and Shop.

King maintains relationships with Bookshop as a reader, as a writer and as a mother and grandmother. Like Franzen, she was a library kid, mostly because her family moved around a lot and they didn't have much money for book purchases, but she wanted bookstores to be a regular part of her children's lives. "My kids grew up in a single house, with bookshelves, and we filled them." She also gives Bookshop abundant praise for maintaining a restroom open to the public for years. "It's a commitment on their part. It sounds like a stupid thing. Who thinks of a toilet in a bookshop? Why should it be Bookshop's responsibility rather than some other place in town? Well, it shouldn't be. But it is. It's part of their community service."

Santa Cruz novelist Elizabeth McKenzie also had a strong relationship with the Capitola Book Café, but when her first book, *Stop That Girl*, came out, Neal Coonerty took a personal interest in it. He slated her for an author appearance. "He gave me this really heartwarming introduction, even though I had never met him before."

"Local literary talent is precious to an independent bookshop," says Coonerty. "It is exciting to see a local writer develop from a solitary hopeful to being part of a writing group to seeing their work find a home in a literary magazine to, finally, featuring their newly published book on our shelves."

McKenzie now travels from city to city on tour to meet her readers, and that means getting to know the nation's indie booksellers. "They are the beating heart of every town you go to," she says.

CHAPTER 5

One Summer in Sligo

The greatest love of Neal Coonerty's life was a love triangle: him, the girl he fancied and William Butler Yeats. Sure, the great Irish poet had been moldering in his grave for close to thirty years when Neal first met teenaged Candy Issenman in Sligo, Ireland. But without Yeats, the lives of these two young people would have never collided. How many people have such a literary pedigree to their meet-cute story?

It was 1968, the year when it seemed that "mere anarchy" was being "loosed upon the world" back home in California. Yeats was there too, at least as inspiration for Joan Didion, who had just published the book that would make her famous, *Slouching Toward Bethlehem*. Neal was on his summer vacation, trying his best to escape the madness of that insane year. He'd just finished his junior year at UC Berkeley, desperate to get away from the ugliness of the protests, the confrontations, the assassinations and the apocalyptic sense of doom that felt particularly heavy on the campus that had been the epicenter of the Free Speech Movement and was a hotbed for student rage against the Vietnam War.

He was the California-born son of an Irish immigrant, touring a foreign country that felt like home. And why shouldn't it? His father had grown up in a town called Sixmilebridge, just to the north of Limerick. His mother was a native Californian, but she was the daughter of two other Irish nationals. Her family came from Donegal on the northern coast.

A kid with those Irish bloodlines, who was actually born on St. Patrick's Day, knows a thing or two about dumb luck, and unless you believe in a supreme being with a taste for mystical Irish poetry, there's no other way to explain how he met Candy. It was one of those moments of serendipity in which any number of small, trivial things could have unfolded differently, and the two would have never met.

She was eighteen, a Jewish girl from Montreal with a jones for Yeats. A few months earlier, back home in Canada, her Harvard brother brought home a poster announcing a Yeats conference to take place in County Sligo, near the childhood home of the famous poet. Her brother suggested that Candy lobby their parents to allow her to go. Reluctantly, her parents relented. "The last thing they wanted was for her to meet somebody, an Irishman or something like that, and get charmed," says Neal today. "So, of course, she comes home and tells them, 'I met the man I'm going to marry.'"

Maybe the poster that Candy saw was the same one that caught Neal's attention as he wandered around the western shore of Ireland. He was a Yeats fan, and knew about the great poet's role in the Irish uprising of 1916, generally not something on the radar of twenty-one-year-old dudes from Los Angeles in the era of *Sgt. Pepper* and *The Smothers Brothers Comedy Hour*. On impulse, he decided to follow Yeats.

He found the conference office, approached the woman behind the desk and announced that he would like a ticket to attend. The woman frowned. Seats at the conference had been reserved months before. Neal, conjuring up his most lost-puppy look, counter-offered. Couldn't he just stand in the back and listen to the lecturers?

Nope, she said, as she continued to open the day's mail. As he muttered "Bummer" to himself and moved toward the door with a Charlie Brown shuffle, the woman just happened to open an envelope from someone announcing they were cancelling their reservation. She called out to Neal absently, "Do you want his spot?"

This is why we must all be grateful we don't have time machines. The moments that forever change the course of your life often will take you by surprise. And only long afterwards are you able to comprehend how delicate those moments are, how all the meaningful ripple effects of your life that followed depended on the precise circumstances of events that you could never hope to control or replicate. Neal never knew, nor could he ever know, exactly who changed their plans not to attend that conference or why. And that person never knew how important that decision was to a man, a family and a community.

Talk about foreshadowing: One of the first things that Neal did after securing his seat at the conference was to visit a Sligo bookshop for a volume of Yeats. A few days later, the conference started with a rowdy reception featuring plenty of all those things you would expect at an Irish party, dancing girls, fight songs and strong drink. That night, Neal's new roommate introduced him to a girl sitting quietly in the middle of the din.

He was bedazzled. She had dark eyes and thick luxurious hair. She told him about her grandfather's love affair with all things Irish and about the scrapbook of poems she had been keeping for years and how Yeats figured in it. Somehow it came up that Candy was related to the famously morose folksinger Leonard Cohen. That got Neal worked up. He wanted to talk to her not about Cohen's music, which he didn't know very well, but about his novel *Beautiful Losers* that had come out the year before. Neal was a big fan of the book. He had even written a paper on it at Berkeley.

She countered that in his first novel, Cohen had disgraced himself. There's a scene in the book, she explained to Neal, in which the protagonist throws a chicken at his mother. "No Jewish boy should ever throw a chicken at his mother," she declared.

Neal was beside himself.

On day two, she boldly suggested that rather than sit through a bunch of tedious lectures, it would more greatly honor the spirit of W.B. Yeats if they hitchhiked to the sites of some of his most well-known poems, Lake Isle of Innisfree, Glencar Falls. Later, Candy asked Neal to accompany her on a bike ride to Knocknarea, a prominent hill outside Sligo, said to be the last resting place of Ireland's mythical Queen Maeve. Candy, who had told Neal she was a year older than she actually was, didn't know how to ride a bicycle very well. She didn't know how to pack a lunch either. "I'm a big guy," says Neal, "and I'm expecting a lunch. And we get there, and she's brought a bunch of raw peas."

It was a very literary romance, surrounded as they were by Yeats, Leonard Cohen and Queen Maeve, in the homeland of Joyce and Wilde and Beckett. Neal Coonerty's romance with Candy Issenman created a template of his life as a husband, father and bookseller. "It was love at first sight," he says now in his Santa Cruz home, a print of the Yeats poem "The Fisherman" on the wall beside him. "It was very intuitive. I mean, this was the right person for me. I believed it, I felt it and I made it happen. I could have hesitated. There are any number of turns that could have happened where things would have turned out differently. Intuition is a very Irish thing. It's taken me down wrong roads at times. But that's part of life too. You just absorb it and learn the lesson: Keep believing in yourself. Keep believing in the romantic story."

★ ★ ★ ★ ★

Talk to Neal Coonerty about books and, sooner or later, he'll admit to you that he's a slow reader. When he was a kid, growing up in the San Fernando Valley, his mother would regularly take Neal and his younger sister Sheila to the public library. The kids would each get a stack of books, but two days later, Sheila was ready to go back, having consumed her books as if they were potato chips. Neal would still be working his way through his first book.

Later, an English teacher at Bishop Alemany High School opened his eyes to foreign film and great literature. At home, he had taken to poring over his family's set of World Book encyclopedias. Still, by the time he got to college at Cal, he had opted to become a political science major in large part because he felt he was too slow a reader to be an English major. He confided in a friend who had won an award for his work in English literature, and the friend said that he too was a slow reader. That convinced Neal to give English a try, entranced with the idea of getting through college reading novels, plays and poetry. He spent his college years in Berkeley hanging out at Cody's and Moe's on Telegraph Avenue, catching up on the American canon: *Main Street* by Sinclair Lewis, Hemingway's *Old Man and the Sea*, Twain's *The Adventures of Huckleberry Finn*. In 1969, he graduated UC Berkeley with a degree in English.

As a kid, Neal was big and athletic, inclined to be outside playing sports rather than inside reading, but his parents had internalized the immigrant's devotion to education as the key to a better life. His mother was an elementary school teacher who had come from an uneducated Irish family and had worked her way to a degree from UC Berkeley. His father had emigrated from Ireland at the age of seventeen, served during World War II and used the GI Bill to get an education after the war. Eventually, Neal's dad became an engineer at the Southern California firm that supplied the engines to the Saturn rockets that put Americans on the moon.

As a college grad, Neal first took steps to follow his mother's career, working briefly as a teacher before convincing himself that he didn't have the skills or temperament to lead a classroom. He found a new role model when he and Candy were married: his father-in-law, who ran a company that manufactured lighting supplies. While Candy was finishing up her degree at Emerson College in Boston, Neal worked at bookstores in Harvard Square and downtown Boston with a notion of learning the ropes of management and budgeting. Candy's father was ready to help the newlyweds by loaning them startup money, and the idea of owning a bookstore became a conscious goal.

Neal's voracious-reader sister Sheila had been part of the first-ever class at UC Santa Cruz in 1965 and Neal had visited the area several times, impressed by its beauty and serenity. It was Sheila, in fact, who told him that Bookshop might be for sale. When Bookshop owner Ron Lau informed him otherwise, a dejected Neal thought that he and Candy would have to turn their attention to San Francisco and finding a bookstore job there. Then, in a similar brush with fate that paralleled Neal's experience trying to get a ticket to the Yeats conference in Sligo back in '68, Lau called him back. He'd changed his mind. The two men entered into negotiations, which Lau insisted on keeping secret. Neal was happy to do so, figuring it would keep away competitors for the business. The negotiations dragged on through the spring and summer of 1973. Candy became pregnant and Neal grew increasingly frustrated with the lack of progress on the deal. Finally, out of work and out of patience, with a baby on the way, Neal wrote Ron a letter withdrawing from negotiations.

The prospect of losing his only bidder caused Lau to refocus and suddenly negotiations were on again. Before it was over, Lau had sold the Coonertys not only the bookstore, but his gorgeous Santa Cruz bungalow as well. He was to remain as the owner of the Bookshop building and the Coonertys' landlord and would spend the next several years pursuing ideas to upgrade his property, most notably building a courtyard near the rear entrance of Bookshop that was to attract a café and other businesses. As far as running and managing the bookstore itself, that was now all in the hands of Neal and Candy. At the age of twenty-seven, Neal Coonerty had his bookstore.

CHAPTER 6

'I Own the Rocking Horse'

I t's only a five-minute stroll from one of Santa Cruz's most sun-bright, postcard-pretty California beaches, but the den in the home of James and Jeanne Wakatsuki Houston is dark and cool, even on the hottest days. The room is redolent of another time, crowded with antique furniture and quiet in a way that I imagine homes used to be before television and air conditioning. I've been a guest in that den dozens of times, on official business and otherwise, and I rank some of those moments among the most sublime of my years as a cultural journalist. As the guy from the local paper, I had license to invite myself over and talk for an hour or two with the Houstons about books, the past, ideas and long dead heroes, all that stuff writers love to talk about. Tall, courtly, cowboy handsome, possessed of the kind of deep oaken speaking voice you would expect Uncle Sam to have, Jim Houston, a protégé of Wallace Stegner, was a gentleman writer, a mischievous spirit in a brawny frame who was always aflame with the passions that drove him, what you might call an emotional geography, in Jim's case, California and Hawaii and the unnameable essence that those two places share. Jeanne was (still is!) whip-smart and radiant, wielding an easy charisma that could melt stone.

The house is a story in its own right, a mighty ramshackle of a thing made of cherrywood and heart redwood with a cupola on top, the subject of one of Jim's most vivid essays. He would go on to write nine novels and about twice that many nonfiction works and win the American Book Award and the Humanitas Prize, and he articulated as well as anyone the psychic and historical dimensions of being a Californian. Much, if not all of that writing took place in the attic office of his Santa Cruz house, including his luminous novel *Snow Mountain Passage*, a heartbreaking fictional take on the famous Donner Party tale. If a house can serve as a muse for a novel, then this is the one.

The Houstons moved into the house as little more than squatters. It was 1962 and the house had been empty for three years. The den's picture window was shattered and whatever furniture left behind had been exposed to the elements for nobody knew how long. The Houstons didn't have much money, so the cheap rent appealed to them. They didn't figure to stay long, but they fell in love with the place and bought the house. In a coincidence that no novelist could get away with, the Houstons later learned that the house had once belonged to the family of Patty Reed, the youngest survivor of the Donner Party, and that some of the artifacts of the Donner Party, including Patty's doll, had been stored in the very same attic where Jim wrote his books about the lure of California and the mythology of its history.

It was inside this house where I sat many times enthralled by Jim's telling of the Donner Party story and its offshoots. These times with Jim and Jeanne were peak experiences for me. Though he was almost thirty years older, I saw a commonality between the two of us. Jim had been born in San Francisco, but his parents were both Southerners. I had been born and raised in the South and had moved west as a young man. We shared a certain temperament that Jeanne recognized as Southern, an introverted nature and a joy in seeing metaphorical connections across geography and history that expressed itself in storytelling. I had come to California for a better life, albeit under circumstances laughably less grim and dramatic than anyone from Patty Reed's generation. Sitting in the Houstons' den was to me like sitting among the ghosts of old California with the one and only man able to conduct the séance.

A decade later, Jim and Jeanne Houston tag-teamed on a book that was to become the most lasting literary legacy of each of them. *Farewell to Manzanar* was a memoir about Jeanne's childhood experience as a Japanese-American detainee in the Manzanar internment camp during World War II, one of the first literary accounts to emerge from that shameful episode. *Farewell to Manzanar* was adapted into a television movie and was adopted into school curricula all over California and the U.S. (The Houstons would later go on to establish the Pacific Rim Film Festival, an annual event in Santa Cruz that cross-pollinated the cultures of California, Hawaii and other Pacific lands through films.) *Manzanar* was where the Houstons' story intersects with the Coonertys. The day that Jim and Jeanne Houston introduced *Manzanar* at a previously scheduled booksigning was also the day that Neal and Candy Coonerty were publicly introduced as Bookshop's new owners.

It was an auspicious first day for the Coonertys. With much of the local literary elite all in the same room, Ron Lau revealed the secret that he had sold the store and warmly introduced Neal Coonerty as the "most normal" person he had ever met. Neal and Candy got to meet the leading lights of the community and from the university. Jeanne Houston remembers the day as one of the first big literary events since she and her husband had moved to

Santa Cruz more than a decade earlier, before even the Hip Pocket opened. "(Bookshop) was the only show in town at that time," she says. "Nobody even knew what it was like to have these kind of big booksignings."

Neal admits today that many of Bookshop's most loyal customers were suspicious of the newcomer. Some of them assumed that the California-born new guy was from the East Coast, not an outrageous assumption given that Neal had first earned his bookselling chops working in Boston. Soon, the wariness faded. Ron Lau remained a familiar face at Bookshop for months after the sale. The Coonertys kept on almost all of the Laus' hires as staff. That included Sharon Lau, who had managed the store for years, and who was more than happy to assume a clerk's role with the Coonertys. She just loved being around books and the bookstore.

By the time of the ownership change, Bookshop's waterbed was gone, but the ethic of hospitality that the Laus had established was picked up by the Coonertys. Retail businesses, even bookstores, were typically not very tolerant of loitering, especially in the hippie era. But there was never any scolding "This is not a library!" signage in Bookshop. As the Laus did before them, the Coonertys were convinced that allowing people to spend time in the store without being hectored to buy or get out was not only the right thing to do but ultimately good for the store's bottom line as well.

A few months after the Coonertys took ownership of Bookshop, their first child was born, a son named Ryan. Two years later came a daughter, Casey. No one has impressions of the prequake Bookshop more deeply embedded in sense memory than the kids who grew up there and have known it their entire lives. Ryan remembers how the basement where the paperbacks and textbooks were shelved had a different smell than the rest of the store. Both remember riding the conveyor belt that Bookshop used to move boxes of new books into the store. Both remember being dispatched to the parking lot to write down license-plate numbers of cars that may have overstayed their two-hour parking limit (though neither remembers their dad ever calling a tow truck).

Casey's earliest memory of the store involves the wooden rocking horse that has become the most tangible symbol of Bookshop's long history. She was four or five when she got into a tussle with another kid on the question of who exactly the rocking horse belonged to. "We just went back and forth, 'No, I own the rocking horse,'" she says. "And I understood, even at that age, that I really did own the rocking horse. It was me staking out my thing: 'This is a part of my family. This is my store.'" History records that Casey won that argument.

The Coonertys' bookselling empire expanded with the purchase of a smaller bookstore called Bookworks in Aptos, ten miles to the east of Santa Cruz. Candy took control at Bookworks and, for several years, the Coonertys' marriage and business partnership was bifurcated between Santa Cruz and Aptos, meeting at the dinner table each evening to share stories and talk business. Much of the Coonerty children's memories of Bookshop as their parents' business were centered around the dining room table.

Family vacations were even centered on books: "We'd go to an independent bookstore wherever we went," says Casey. "We took boxes of books with us on our vacations. It was like, 'Hey, let's go someplace far away and read as a family!'"

Growing up among surfers and athletes, young Ryan did not always feel that his family's bookstore was the most awesome place to hang out. "You don't, as a kid, realize how cool it was to grow up in a bookstore. I was always asking my parents, 'Why couldn't you have owned a pizza place or sporting goods store?'"

What the children might not have appreciated in the 1970s and '80s was the burgeoning scene centered at Bookshop and Ron Lau's adjoining courtyard. Taking the place of the Catalyst as

Bookshop's neighboring literary watering hole was Caffe Pergolesi, which soon became the home of something called Penny University, a kind of weekly salon of intellectuals and artists run by maverick UC Santa Cruz faculty members Paul Lee, Mary Holmes and Page Smith. After Pergolesi closed (to emerge later in a new space across town), the celebrated modern dancer Tandy Beal (who happened to be married to composer Jon Scoville) entered into a partnership with Neal Coonerty to operate a new café behind Bookshop to be known as Café Zinho, which became well known for its live music performances, most memorably the Santa Cecilia Society doing Gregorian chants on Sunday mornings.

Poetry found a special foothold in Santa Cruz, and the Coonertys, who owed their marriage to Yeats, contributed to its flourishing. A rich homegrown poetry ecosystem developed from such nationally known writers as the New York-born ex-boxer Morton Marcus, who followed Jim Houston to Santa Cruz, and the San Francisco printer and poet William Everson, who in his later years grew his hair out Rip Van Winkle-style and was widely known as "Brother Antoninus." UC Santa Cruz poet George Hitchcock developed a reputation as one of the country's most significant maverick publishers of poetry with his journal *Kayak*. (However, he wasn't the most famous Hitchcock to call the area his home; that would be a fellow by the name of Alfred Hitchcock, whose ranch and retreat was in neighboring Scotts Valley.)

Was Bookshop a driver of the literary renaissance of the time? Or merely along for the ride? That's impossible to measure. UC Santa Cruz and nearby Cabrillo College were obviously seedbeds, offering landing spots for many writers as teachers, but would-be writers were crawling up and down the coast of California in those years, looking for communities in which to make a life. And Bookshop served as a cultural nexus for writers and readers, and was beginning to develop an image as "Santa Cruz's living room." As a UC undergrad, novelist Elizabeth McKenzie approached Bookshop as a pilgrim might approach a cathedral. "I remember thinking that Bookshop Santa Cruz was so cool that I was scared to go into it. There was nothing mean or intimidating about it, quite the opposite. I just felt like the people who worked there were gods."

Bookshop would occasionally attract brand-name authors for visits, such as pioneering science-fiction writer Robert Heinlein, who moved to the Santa Cruz area in the 1960s and lived there for twenty years, and Frank Herbert, the former *San Francisco Examiner* editor who created the *Dune* series. Early on in his tenure, Neal Coonerty adopted Walt Whitman as Bookshop's icon, converting a self-portrait woodcut from *Leaves of Grass* into part of Bookshop's logo.

Throughout the '70s and '80s, poetry readings were common, drawing large crowds and making Santa Cruz a destination for prominent poets from out of town. Bookshop's Patrick O'Connell arranged a series of readings in the early '80s featuring such heavyweights as Galway Kinnel, Robert Bly, Michael McClure and Carolyn Forché. O'Connell was a Southern California native who had lived in a spiritual community in India for a decade. He wandered into Bookshop in the late 1970s at a time when it seemed everybody was either quoting from "Hotel California" or imitating Horshack's honking laugh from *Welcome Back Kotter.* O'Connell was new to town, just back from India, and he asked a Bookshop employee if they carried a V.S. Naipul book that had been banned in India. O'Connell also asked if the store might be hiring. As a matter of fact, yes. The person responsible for overseeing the religion and spirituality section of the store was leaving. Today, close to forty years later, O'Connell still works at Bookshop, as a manager, a trusted eminence and a consigliere to the Coonerty family. For years, he has been doing most of the hiring at Bookshop, as well as the training and evaluation of other employees. He has worked with hundreds of people at the store, most of whom love books because they maintain a rich interior life and value curiosity, empathy, imagination, humor, the precision and expressiveness of language and the unique sensation of psycho-emotional transport and uplift that only storytelling and poetry can reach.

Like most jobs that look cool on paper, managing a bookstore has its share of tedium. But O'connell likes to remind his new hires that connecting a reader with a book is both a social act and a political act, and they are potential conduits in transforming someone's life in a way that only a book can. "It may amuse them for an afternoon, or it may change their lives," he says. "The fact that we are an agent in that process is to me the importance of what being a bookseller is all about. And it's not always easy to remember that."

In O'Connell's years at Bookshop he struck up friendships with many writers, including influential feminist poet Adrienne Rich, who moved to Santa Cruz in the early 1980s, around the time *Ms.* Magazine was dubbing Santa Cruz a "feminist utopia." When Rich won the 2004 National Book Critics Circle Award, her publisher called Bookshop to find someone to deliver a congratulatory bottle of Champagne to her home. O'Connell happened to answer the phone, and he happened to know where the poet lived. He made the delivery. Rich was a friend and supporter of Bookshop until her death, in 2012.

In 1980, Bookshop Santa Cruz suddenly had its first significant rival as the primary indie bookstore in its market. Five miles to the east, the Capitola Book Café opened, going after much of the same customer base. In future years, Neal Coonerty would develop a reputation for confrontational defiance against rival bookstores, but the Book Café was a different animal. Over the decades, the two bookstores enjoyed a friendly rivalry. If one store could not fulfill a customer request, it often directed the customer to the other store. Bookshop was the established institution and it enjoyed a prime downtown location, but the Book Café had a coffee bar inside the store, still a novel idea in those days, and a large theater-like marquee above its front entrance.

Today, Bookshop regularly brings in many of the most prominent novelists, journalists and authors in publishing: Stephen King, Deepak Chopra, David Sedaris, Dave Eggers … we could go on all day. Much of the credit for putting this otherwise sleepy beach community on the radar of the big New York publishing houses actually goes to the Capitola Book Café. Seeking an edge in the marketplace, the Book Café began to invite big-name authors to its store. Among the early writers to visit were cultural historian Riane Eisler (*The Chalice and the Blade*) and novelist Amy Tan (*The Joy Luck Club*).

Radio journalist, and one-time *Jeopardy* contestant, Eric Schoeck played a key role in attracting heavyweight names, first as an interviewer and then working as the events coordinator at the Book Café. "All I ever heard from authors was, 'I just had the best interview I've ever had,'" says Richard Lange, who preceded Schoeck as the Book Café's events coordinator. "They would say, 'This guy read the whole book and asked excellent questions.' And so, enough people went back to New York and said, maybe it's not the biggest audience, but authors sure like it there."

Before long, the Book Café was commonly part of the book tours put together by the Big Five publishers. "You'd see an itinerary for an author," says Lange. "And it would say, 'New York, Minneapolis, Seattle, San Francisco, Capitola.' Anybody not from California is thinking, 'Oh, they probably meant Washington, D.C., they just bumbled the word Capitol.' Here we were, 9,000 people in Capitola, up against the biggest markets in the country."

Laurie R. King moved to Santa Cruz in 1974, shortly after the Coonertys took ownership at Bookshop. King was a regular customer at Bookshop. She would often bring her kids in to spend time in Bookshop's children's section, but it was the Book Café that first lent her a hand when she was an unknown aspiring novelist. When she won an Edgar Award for her first novel in 1994, she turned to Book Café to celebrate. "After that," she says, "I always tried to do my first event on a new book at the Book Café. It was all about loyalty for me."

It was during the '70s and '80s that Santa Cruz also began to blossom culturally as a haven for left-of-center tolerance of new ideas and alternative lifestyles. On the night that Richard Nixon announced he was resigning the presidency, the Caffe Pergolesi, behind Bookshop, spontaneously offered drinks on the house. A few years later, when Nixon released his autobiography, Bookshop sold it for the per-pound price of bologna, the first of many similar attention-getting stunts that Neal Coonerty initiated. (At the price of bologna, the Nixon book was sold at a loss, but the corresponding media publicity made it all worth it, from Coonerty's point of view.)

Coonerty joined the effort of other independent booksellers in Northern California to force publishers to stop giving sweetheart deals to big chains at the expense of indies. In the emerging Santa Cruz political scene, he looked to play the go-between among conservative old-line retailers and the emerging progressive constituency that had been established since the founding of the university. He understood and experienced the day-to-day anxieties of the merchants, but he was also simpatico with the university crowd and the granola culture that had taken hold in Santa Cruz.

By the end of the '80s, the shady downtown Pacific Garden Mall was beginning to show its age. Many felt the downtown was become seedy, thanks in large part to what were called "UTEs," or "undesirable transient elements," an issue that downtown businesses like Bookshop confronted every day. Homelessness and rents were both on the rise. It looked like the 1990s were going to be challenging times.

CHAPTER 7

10/17/89

For those of us living in Northern California, October 1989 was shaping up to be a memorable time: The baseball gods had smiled on us. The Bay Area was already lucky enough to have two big-league baseball teams, the San Francisco Giants and Oakland Athletics. To have them square off that month in the Bay Bridge World Series, baseball's best-of-seven championship series, was just too much good fortune to process, like winning both the Nobel in physics and *People*'s Sexiest Man Alive at the same time. One is shocking. Both, that's just absurd.

Santa Cruz is Giants country. That means 1989 would have been a big deal no matter who the Giants played. In their tenure in Oakland, the A's had ridden the karmic wheel from world-beaters (three straight championships in the '70s) to bottom feeders and back again. By contrast, the Giants had been forever stuck in mediocrity. Before '89, they had played in the World Series just once since they had moved to San Francisco from New York. And they lost. Then came a couple of decades of watching their reviled rivals, the Los Angeles Dodgers, play in the Series a half dozen times. Yes, the Giants had Willie Mays, but L.A. had the rings.

Then as now, A's fans were a proud but distinct minority in Santa Cruz. In '89, they were no less dialed in on the Bay Bridge showdown, and they were no less hungry for glory. The star-studded A's had played in the World Series the year before, but had lost in appalling fashion (curse thee and thine offspring, Kirk Gibson) to the much less talented Dodgers. Even for less ferociously partisan fans, including those who bought those funky ballcaps with both the A's and Giants logos on them, the matchup between the young and fearless Giants and the brawny and charismatic A's was must-watch TV. So in October 1989 the Giants and A's lifted a lot of hearts in Santa Cruz. But they also saved some lives. Literally.

One of the most devastating earthquakes in Northern California history struck on October 17, 1989, just minutes before the first pitch of the first World Series game to be played in San Francisco since 1962. When the quake hit, the shops and sidewalks of downtown Santa Cruz were not as populated as you might otherwise expect on a warm, jasmine-scented fall afternoon. Three people died in collapsing buildings in downtown Santa Cruz that day, far fewer than could have been expected to perish under normal circumstances. Instead, many who might have been hanging around downtown on a normal day made the trip to Candlestick Park to see the game or were already home when the quake hit, mixing up their margaritas and making their guacamole while waiting for the first pitch.

I had just finished my very first day as a daily newspaper reporter. A couple of weeks earlier, I had been hired by the tiny *Gilroy Dispatch*, in the self-anointed Garlic Capital of the World, less than twenty miles from the epicenter of the quake on a ridge known as Loma Prieta. That first day had not been fun. I had started a day later than I was expected to, and I suspect my section editor was already wondering if she had hired a turkey. I wasn't sure what to wear or how to act in a newsroom. I had moved from Humboldt County in the far north of California, more than three hundred fifty miles away. I was already wondering if I had made a terrible mistake. At least there was the game to look forward to. When my editor bolted early to go watch, I slipped away too.

I was on the 101 freeway listening to the pregame on the radio when the steering column to my dumpy Subaru wagon suddenly became disconnected from my front axle, or so it felt. I pulled over, marveling at the coincidence that every other driver around also had broken their drivetrain at the exact same moment. What are the odds? When I finally figured out it had been an earthquake, I headed straight back to the newspaper office, which was dark and empty (there was no electricity for hours). There, backlit by the late-afternoon sunlight streaming in through the window, was the *Dispatch*'s city editor, a massive, stubby-fingered volcano of a man who I had spent the previous eight hours hiding from. He was your stereotypical Ed Asner-style newspaper lifer but in the darkened cave of the office, he looked to me more like the alpha male on Cell Block C at San Quentin. And I felt like Pee-wee Herman. He didn't even know my name. Still, he barked out a half-dozen orders, running down streets and place names where I was to go to collect quotes and information. I had no clue where any of these places were, and even less inclination to ask him to elaborate. A weird, weird night was getting even weirder. When it came to the Bay Bridge World Series, I learned that moment, like millions of others in Northern California, one of life's most disorienting lessons: One minute, baseball is everything. The next, it's nothing.

Downtown Santa Cruz was about ten miles from the quake's epicenter, and it was walloped as badly as any other town in Northern California. More than three dozen commercial buildings were leveled by or later demolished because of the quake, including the iconic old Cooper House, the symbol of Santa Cruz. Among the crippled properties was the Bookshop building. The Loma Prieta earthquake should have destroyed Bookshop Santa Cruz, as it did many other businesses. In a physical sense, that's exactly what happened.

O'Connell, who normally worked until five, was among many who knocked off early to catch the World Series. Once at home, he noticed that his housemate's dog was "going crazy" in the backyard. A few minutes later, some unseen giant picked up his house and shook it.

Like most native Californians, O'Connell was born factory-equipped with an intuitive inner gauge when it came to earthquakes. Right away, he knew that this one was beyond any he had ever experienced. He quickly returned to downtown Santa Cruz and parked near Mission Plaza, which is situated on a bluff overlooking the north end of downtown. From that vantage point, he could see that the second floor of the north-facing wall of the Bookshop building had peeled away. What he didn't know yet, but was soon to learn, was the wall from the bookstore had collapsed in on the neighboring business, the Santa Cruz Coffee Roasting Company. Two of the employees working that day at Coffee Roasting were unaccounted for. By nightfall, the building would become a search-and-rescue site. O'Connell was there that night for hours, as the scene became a vigil for the missing employees.

If you were in the line of sight of downtown Santa Cruz that day, you would not have been able to see much. The area was obscured not by smoke from fires (though one house adjacent to downtown did catch fire) but from clouds of yellowish dust from so many suddenly collapsed buildings. One woman said the dust was so thick in the first few minutes, she couldn't see her hand in front of her face. Then came the distinct mildewy smell from the trapped gases of the downed buildings. In the hours after the quake, when police had fenced off the area, a news photographer remembered the sound of falling brick and broken water mains providing an eerie soundtrack to the ruin all around him.

Ryan Coonerty, the fifteen-year-old son of Bookshop's owners, was changing clothes after enduring an unusually hot day at football practice at Santa Cruz High School. He and his buddies were not yet old enough to drive legally but, as soon as the quake hit, they borrowed a car to cruise around town anyway, figuring the cops would be too busy with other things to notice them. They were right on that score.

Ryan's dad, Neal, was nowhere near downtown Santa Cruz for reasons that had nothing to do with baseball. He had a doctor's appointment in San Jose, part of the South Bay megalopolis beyond the Santa Cruz Mountains that Santa Cruzans tend to lump together as "over the hill."

Neal Coonerty, a lifelong Californian, knew his earthquakes. He was a kid growing up in the San Fernando Valley north of Los Angeles when the 1952 Tehachapi earthquake struck (magnitude 7.3, the second strongest quake in California in the twentieth century, behind only the epic 1906 San Francisco quake). "It was the middle of the night," he says, "and I can remember feeling the bed moving across the floor and my dad coming in to see if I was all right." Years later, in his early days as Bookshop's owner, he remembers eating lunch at a downtown restaurant and watching a plate-glass window wobble ominously during a minor shaker.

What happened on October 17 was of an entirely different character. He felt certain that it was epicentered in the Santa Clara Valley, where he was at the time. "My first thought was, I wonder if they felt it in Santa Cruz." Electricity went down throughout the region immediately and phone service was spotty as well. Coonerty went to the home of his sister Roseanne in nearby Los Altos. He was finally able to connect with his wife, Candy, at the Coonertys' Santa Cruz home, where the chimney had collapsed.

As the scope of the disaster was becoming apparent, Coonerty's first focus was on the welfare of his family, Candy, Ryan and his middle-school daughter, Casey. His parents and his in-laws also lived in town and he was preoccupied that everyone was safe and accounted for. Highway 17, the famously treacherous connector between Santa Cruz and San Jose, was quickly closed after the quake, forcing Coonerty onto pokey, two-lane Highway 9 to get home. There wasn't much traffic, he remembered, but the quake had thrown debris onto the roadway in several places, making it a long slog. It was while crawling home on Highway 9 that Coonerty heard a radio report from the local AM station KSCO that referenced Bookshop. Judging only by the intact façade – not even the windows were broken – the radio reporter announced that Bookshop looked OK.

In fact, a desperate drama was unfolding on the site as first responders worked to recover the bodies of the two employees of the Santa Cruz Coffee Roasting Company who had been buried by the bricks of Bookshop's wall. Coonerty was unaware of any of that. After he finally got home, well after dark, he was up most of the night, assessing the damage to his home and calming his daughter through the night's many aftershocks. At first light, he made his way downtown, figuring there was inevitable damage at the bookstore, that he'd spend all day picking up and reshelving books. However, he was unprepared for what he encountered. As he approached the back door of the business, he was stopped by a Santa Cruz police officer who told him no one was allowed inside. "That told me something was very wrong," he says.

He immediately noticed large cracks in the back of the building. He then saw an enormous U-shaped hole in the wall to his left and knew that his business had been crippled, maybe fatally so. It was only then that Coonerty became aware of the drama that had been going on at Coffee Roasting. The night before, rescue workers dug through the bricks in an effort to find the bodies of employees Shawn McCormick and Robin Ortiz, but the numerous aftershocks compelled the workers to retreat; much of the unreinforced brick wall was still standing and thus capable of collapsing, causing potentially more injury or death. Yet friends of the missing coffeehouse employees were vocally upset at the delays, and the scene became fraught with emotion and confrontation. Under the circumstances, few people were thinking about Neal Coonerty's troubles, even if the ruins of Bookshop made it all too apparent to Coonerty himself. Given that loans on the bookstore were collateralized with his house, it appeared that he was poised to lose everything.

* * * * *

In the Hollywood movie that will surely never be made of this story, the image on the movie poster would be a bearded, burly Neal Coonerty a few days after the quake, standing on the sidewalk in downtown Santa Cruz, wearing a hardhat and two flashlights duct-taped around each forearm, looking like some lock-key nine-year-old kid pretending to be a superhero. But this was no fun and games. The stakes for Coonerty's personal and professional life could not have been higher. The mood was tense, the crowd around him somber, emotional. Standing next to him was a sleep-deprived volunteer, acting as a city official, looking at her watch, poised to give the signal.

The fate of Bookshop quickly became a secondary concern in the quake's aftermath. Two young lives had been snuffed out on site. Although its façade looked intact, the beloved bookstore had suffered grave damage. Indeed, it had been red-tagged for demolition by the roving band of structural engineers brought in to decide the fate of each building in the area. Red-tagged buildings had been deemed far too dangerous to enter, particularly given the frequent aftershocks, but many downtown merchants had insisted they be given a chance to retrieve some personal effects from their businesses. The suddenness of the quake had caused people to leave behind their purses, coats, wallets and other valuables. In the days before widespread computer record keeping, many businesses, like Bookshop, also had essential records and documents in folders and file cabinets. The compromise was straightforward. The owner of each red-tagged business would be allowed access to his or her building for fifteen minutes only, for one person to collect and gather whatever they needed in a building with no light or electricity and with unknown dangers and hazards. There was a chance, who was to say how remote, that he or she would not come out alive.

Coonerty was in his mid-forties at the time. He was a bookseller with a decidedly Falstaffian physique, not some obstacle-course-running athlete. This weird stunt, which even today sounds like something from a Japanese game show, could not have been anything he thought he'd ever be called on to do. He had with him only a crude diagram that showed him roughly where to find specific items belonging to his employees. It was an absurd situation, but considering that bodies had only recently been pulled from the building and the chance that an aftershock might bring it down on his inadequately protected head, Coonerty was in no mood to laugh it off.

The moment came, and the bookseller dashed into the store. Hundreds of fallen books, *Megatrends* mingling with Michener, John Irving on top of Irving Wallace, covered the floor creating a minefield of potential twisted ankles or falls, particularly for a man in a hurry not used to timed tests of physical agility. The only light in the store was the daylight streaming in through the collapsed wall, but the building had a basement. That's where Coonerty's office was, and where the staff kept their personal belongings. That's where he was headed. The stairs closest to the front of the store were impassable and Coonerty had to go to the back of the store to access the only other staircase to the basement, then had to reverse course in the pitch-black basement, wielding his arm lights, to reach his office, hearing the tick-tock of his fifteen minutes evaporate with every step. He retrieved what he could, stacking boxes on the sidewalk, winded and sweating, while a crowd looked on. He was even able to drag out an antique English desk that had been right by the front door.

The woman with the watch gently informed him that his time was up, although as he remembers it today, he was given more than fifteen minutes. Still, he headed back in, telling her over his shoulder, "This will be a quick trip." At that moment, Coonerty was overcome by the painful realization that he was spending his final moments inside the bookstore that he had nurtured and sustained for almost his entire adult life. He had achieved a dream, having purchased the bookstore at the age of twenty-seven. His marriage, his family, his community, his livelihood, his very purpose were all deeply entwined in Bookshop Santa Cruz. This thing is going away, he thought, and I'm not going to be able to save it.

"It was an emotional situation," he says. "I thought, if I'm going to start over, or even if I'm not, I need to have at least one symbol of the bookstore." He moved to the store's children's area and picked up a rustic wooden rocking horse. A couple of generations of Santa Cruz children, including his own son and daughter, had rocked away on that horse. This, he thought, was worth saving. When he emerged, finally, back outside carrying the rocking horse and one last box of financial records, he thought what everyone else gathered that day thought: Bookshop Santa Cruz was gone.

Chapter 8

Our Bookstore

Those who love bookstores will tell you that a well-stocked, well-curated community bookstore is of a different nature than, say, a great local hardware store, or grocery store, however much the latter is cherished in any given community. Unlike a well-made hammer or an artisanal loaf of bread, a book isn't usually treasured for its own thingness. A book is merely a medium that carries ideas, stories, lessons, declarations, instructions, the bulk of accumulated knowledge and wisdom across time and space. That's why an independent, locally owned bookstore can so effectively mirror its community. An independent bookstore's social, political and moral values are often more readily on display than in other businesses. It's why bookstores often generate the kind of goodwill and loyalty that other businesses can't quite muster. Neal Coonerty knew this better than most, at least intellectually. After Loma Prieta, he learned it emotionally.

After his fifteen-minute dash through his red-tagged bookstore,

Coonerty, his family, his employees and customers all had to face the reality that Bookshop Santa Cruz was gone. But Coonerty knew he had to act in some way, to exhaust all other possibilities, before he could walk off into a new life. With a sense of Irish fatalism, he sought solace in the dimmest of silver linings: "I will say, honestly, there was a certain kind of relief," he says. "If the Bookshop was ever going to go under because business was bad, your failure would be on the front page of the (Santa Cruz) *Sentinel.* If you went under because an earthquake hit, then you're off the hook. It wasn't your fault. You could start over. You weren't a failed businessman."

Coonerty carefully reviewed his options. He resisted surrendering to a circumstance that many people might chalk up to cosmic fate. A certain kind of survival instinct, familiar to most small businesspeople, kicked in. Yet he also knew that he needed to keep a cool head and develop a realistic vision of where he wanted to go. "I kept thinking, 'I have to move forward, but I have no room to make a mistake. One error and it's all over.'"

He found out the name of the structural engineer who was in charge of the demolition of the Bookshop building. Through a mutual friend, he was able to contact the man. Coonerty told the engineer, "Look, I know you're going to pull down the Bookshop building. I have two things to ask. First, could you schedule it for the end of the run of the other demolitions? And two, can you do me the favor of walking through the building and then tell me if I could possibly get my inventory out? If you say it's just too dangerous and unsafe for anyone to go in there, then I'll accept my fate. But if you tell me it's OK, will you allow me to tell the city manager?"

The engineer said that he would call the next day. He didn't. At nightfall, an anxious Coonerty called him back. The engineer's assessment gave Coonerty some breathing room. If he could prop up the roof with a beam or two and build a kind of tunnel for entrance and exit, the building would probably hold, for a while anyway. Coonerty was convinced that if he could get his books out of the building, he could somehow continue on. Even with that bit of daylight, there were still daunting logistical tasks: How to convince the city to go along with the plan, how to build a tunnel in and out of the building, how to get thousands of books out of the building and what to do with them once they were out. Still, Coonerty took the plan to Dick Wilson, Santa Cruz's city manager. Wilson looked at the plans and, once he had made the modifications the engineer suggested, he gave Coonerty two days – daylight hours only – to get his inventory out. On top of that, every person who went into the bookstore had to sign a waiver acknowledging that entering the building was potentially fatal, and if it were to collapse, there would be no rescue efforts.

The next day Coonerty went on the air at the local public radio station in Santa Cruz to inform the community what was happening with the bookstore. Of course, he had another motive: He was looking for volunteers to help with the inventory recovery effort. Many of Bookshop's twenty employees, having been inside the store during the earthquake, were understandably hesitant to venture back inside, and Coonerty respected their choices. But even if they were all gung-ho, that still left him short-handed to carry out thousands of books, including the newly received inventory for the upcoming holiday season.

"The thinking was, let's solve the problem that was in front of us," says Coonerty. "The larger concept of 'Will we make it?' 'Will we survive?' got immediately replaced by 'What do we have to do today? What do we have to do this hour to move forward?'"

After a makeshift tunnel made from railroad ties had been constructed at Bookshop's back entrance, the day of the big book evacuation arrived. Neal and Candy got up early and made their way to Bookshop, not knowing what to expect. Coming down the hill from their home toward downtown, they saw a huge crowd outside the store. More than four hundred people – friends, readers, customers, community members – showed up willing to sign the "buried alive" waiver to help the Coonertys retrieve their books.

Those who were there that day remember a palpable sense of purpose. The sobering fact that two people had died on the site put a damper on any kind of celebratory mood. No one was certain that the crippled building would not collapse while the book rescue was going on, and the waiver was somewhat less than reassuring on that score. Yet, many people had been frustrated by a sense of helplessness since the quake. Here was something they could do to help. A task of physical labor like this one, with a patina of danger, of life-and-death seriousness, of limited time, is not something that many contemporary Americans experience much. The volunteers were motivated by that sense of mission and drama, and they got to work with enthusiasm.

Other businesses pitched in with vital help and supplies as well. A vegetable packer from the nearby strawberry-rich fields of the Pajaro Valley offered dozens of much-needed cardboard boxes. A local leather tannery loaned out an industrial roller that allowed boxes of books to be moved out of the bookstore, conveyor-belt style, more efficiently. A trucking company brought over a semitrailer in which to store the books. A friend who once ran a department store showed up with his forklift. Someone else contributed hardhats. Even Coonerty's competitors appeared that day, including the owners and staff of the Capitola Book Café, as well as employees of the county's library system.

A kind of bucket brigade was set up as a small number of specially designated workers inside the building would pass along the books, many of which were coated in dust and debris, to others waiting outside. Each book was assessed for damage, cleaned off as well as possible, sorted and boxed for storage in the trailer. The work was long and repetitive, but with an autumnal chill in the air (a welcome contrast to the blistering hot afternoon of the quake), the somber occasion turned to moments of levity and the volunteers experienced a sense of meaningful camaraderie that for many ripened into elation.

Today, Coonerty still gets emotional looking back on that weekend. For years after, new hires at Bookshop would hear the story as if it were part of their orientation package. When the Coonertys say that the community saved their bookstore, they are speaking literally. "A community doesn't come out to help a store proprietor," says poet and teacher Patrice Vecchione, who grew up in Santa Cruz and was there moving books both days. "A community comes out to restore something that matters to them. This was *our* bookstore."

By late Sunday afternoon, the bucket brigade had gotten all the inventory out of the damaged Bookshop building. The volunteers had gone home. Neal Coonerty decided to go back into his bookstore one more time. He called to his teenage son Ryan to join him. Ryan had watched dumbfounded for two days as strangers handled his dad's books with meticulous care. In the darkness of the store as they moved downstairs, he expected his dad to say something poignant, to try to sum up his life as a bookseller or to articulate what the previous ten days had been like for him. Instead, Neal picked up a couple of bricks from the floor, handed one to his son and gestured toward the big windows in his office and Bookshop's accounting office.

"So there we were, father and son, just throwing bricks through windows," says Ryan, almost three decades later. "I often think about that. He was so moved by the community being there for him. His business had just been saved. I can't imagine the emotional strain of that day and the weeks leading up to it for him. Yet he could still figure out a way to break the rules a little bit, to still be a risk-taker, to just not take it all so seriously."

At home, the Coonertys' answering machine was jammed with phone calls from bookseller friends from around the country. Under the aegis of the Northern California Independent Booksellers Association, other independent booksellers established a fund from which Bookshop could pay its employees during the crisis. Some of the major publishers that Bookshop did business with either restructured or forgave altogether Bookshop's outstanding debts.

The following week, the Coonertys turned again to the community. Bookshop needed some working capital and Neal had an idea. Since the earthquake, the staff had often convened at the Coonertys' home, usually on the front lawn or in the back yard (many people were still wary of being indoors, considering the aftershocks). Coonerty decided to invite the community to his house. He went door to door to get permission from his neighbors to close off the street for the day. Then, he announced a book sale for the purpose of raising money so that Bookshop could reopen. He asked book lovers not only to come to buy books but to bring books to donate as well. "Five good books" became the rallying cry. And people responded.

The atmosphere at the book sale was much lighter than it was at the book rescue. The somber vibe gave way to a more celebratory mood. Coonerty was not shy about using the word "party." One of Santa Cruz's most prominent musicians performed. An emcee kept the proceedings lively. People streamed in carrying books and left carrying more books. Some people brought five of their most treasured books, donated them, and immediately repurchased them. Some brought five books, others brought fifty. As the recipient of all this largesse, Coonerty was insistent that the community had now earned a kind of spiritual (if not legal) ownership of the store and that he was merely a steward of a community touchstone.

Throughout the extended post-earthquake melodrama, let's remember that Coonerty did not meet a kindly old angel trying to earn his wings. He did not run in a panic through the streets of Santa Cruz in the snow. He did not get to experience an alternate-reality Santa Cruz in which he never existed. But the weekend of the book rescue, and to a lesser degree the book sale, was clearly his George Bailey moment, when an individual's faith that the community he serves will be there for him in a time of crisis is rewarded. Still, the situation was pretty far afield from *It's a Wonderful Life*. Four hundred volunteers showing up ready to give their time and labor is a wonderful image, though it alone ensured nothing to the survival of Bookshop Santa Cruz. That would come only through institutional and political decisions made by the city's government and business elites.

In the wake of Loma Prieta, business and political interests formed an unwieldy thirty-six-member committee that came to be known as Vision Santa Cruz. There were dozens of businesses other than Bookshop that were displaced from damaged buildings or otherwise crippled by the earthquake. It might have seemed prudent at the time to minimize the city's liability by clearing out the downtown district altogether in order to rebuild the damaged buildings. But Vision Santa Cruz considered it crucial to somehow keep the displaced retailers in business and keep shoppers coming to downtown. Otherwise they might arrive at a point with a downtown full of new buildings and no businesses to occupy them. As a result, the city erected in the downtown parking lots a number of "pavilions," temporary structures of uniform size that resembled beige-colored circus tents. Soon enough, they became known as "the tents."

By the time the Bookshop building had come down, the Coonertys had moved into one of these pavilions. They had set aside a weekend to move the books from storage into their new tent. But so many volunteers showed up, they had finished moving the books by Friday afternoon. The store was open for business by Saturday.

As a marketing move, Neal and Candy decided to embrace the concept of the pavilions. The interior of the new "tent" was about the same size as the old store, so the Coonertys painstakingly attempted to re-create the exact layout and look of the store. A large sign featuring the Bookshop Santa Cruz logo was purposefully altered; the "shop" was crossed out with the word "tent" written above it, like a teacher correcting a spelling error on a student's paper. The "Booktent Santa Cruz" first opened the day after Thanksgiving, 1989, the unofficial opening day of the holiday shopping season. A few days earlier, Highway 17, Santa Cruz's lifeline to the greater Bay Area, had also opened for the first time since the quake.

What followed was yet another Jimmy Stewart moment for Neal and Candy Coonerty. Both locals and out-of-towners flooded into downtown Santa Cruz to show support for the displaced merchants. The Booktent was filled with people ready to spend. Lines to buy books stretched outside the door and down the block. "To buy a book, people had to carry it outside the store and stand in line for twenty minutes," Neal remembers. "It would have been so easy to steal a book. You could have just walked away with it. But people didn't do that. They stood in line and bought books."

The owner of the Bookshop building, Ron Lau, had earthquake insurance, one of the few downtown property owners who did. Buoyed by the response from the community to the Booktent opening, Coonerty figured that he could survive a year in the tent, and by the following Christmas, he'd be back in business in a new building, and the new normal would again resemble the old normal. He was wrong. Just as his pessimism in the days after the earthquake turned out to be unfounded, his optimism was off the mark too.

CHAPTER 9

Booktent Santa Cruz

There is no superhero in the comic-book canon known as "The Bookseller." We can't even imagine what such a superhero's costume might look like, beyond the orthopedic shoes and smudgy eyeglasses. Her superpower? That's the easy part: mind reading. Think of a book, approach her with "Hi, I'm looking for that book? By that, um, guy? Y'know what I'm talking 'bout? I think the color of the cover is blue, or blue-ish." The Mighty Thor would look at you like a dead fish. The Bookseller, though? She'll have it in your hands in minutes.

Neal Coonerty's mad dash into a potentially deadly building notwithstanding, booksellers aren't usually called to do physically heroic things. Navy SEALs they aren't, but sometimes courage in the bookselling business goes well beyond the willingness to face unpleasant emails, or confront a shoplifter. Sometimes you have to act on principle and realistically expect to bleed for it. And we don't mean that metaphorically. Just ask the staff of Cody's Books in Berkeley, circa 1989.

Cody's was a landmark in the history of American independent bookstores and, for fifty years, played a key role in Berkeley's ongoing evolution into a bastion for free speech and intellectual freedom. In the fall of '88, Salman Rushdie's new novel *The Satanic Verses*, which reimagined the life of the Islamic prophet Muhammad, was first published in the U.K. What followed was book burnings, bomb threats and the banning of the book in several countries around the world. A few months after the book's U.S. publication, it was condemned by that famous literary critic Iran's Ayatollah Khomeini, who we can say with a fair amount of certainty didn't get his copy at Cody's. Khomeini issued a fatwa against Rushdie, which resulted in several failed assassination attempts.

In Berkeley, despite the fact that several major bookstore chains had already pulled the novel off their shelves, Cody's continued to display *The Satanic Verses* in its front window. And on February 28, the store paid the price. In the darkest hours of the early morning, someone threw a firebomb through that window. That was scary enough, but while the employees were cleaning up the next day, an undetonated pipe bomb was found "rolling around the floor in the poetry section," as store owner Andy Ross puts it.

Selling books for a living rarely entails facing down life-or-death situations, but in this instance, the employees of Cody's had to decide whether carrying Rushdie's book was worth the threat of injury or death. Then, in the heat of the spotlight from the national news media, they voted unanimously not to fold to the intimidation. When the bookstore reopened, *The Satanic Verses* was still available.

That moment had a profound effect on young Phyllis Cohen. When *The Satanic Verses* was published in the U.S., Phyllis was seventeen years old growing up in the East Bay suburb of San

Leandro. She was a bookish kid and whenever she was in Berkeley, a half hour's drive to the north in light traffic, she always found a way to spend some time at Cody's Books. She had a prime seat to witness Cody's finest moment. Today, Phyllis is a bookseller in her own right, running a small bookshop in the heart of the Latin Quarter of Paris. The bookstore is called Berkeley Books. Soon after she opened for business in 2006, Phyllis, in an echo of a defiant act more than fifteen years earlier, put a first edition copy of *The Satanic Verses* in her front window.

Running a bookstore in Paris is an almost laughably romantic notion, a backyard-hammock daydream of the Sweet Life for many of us, reinforced by such twinkly City of Light fantasies as the commercial juggernaut novel *The Little Paris Bookshop*. But Phyllis told the story of what Cody's meant to her in the spring of 2016, just six months after a coordinated terror attack by the radical Islamic State in Paris killed 130 people, and a little more than a year after the deadly Charlie Hebdo killings, which were, let's face it, a variation on the theme of what animated the threats aimed at *The Satanic Verses*. Aside from the horrifying violence, the attacks have had crippling effects on small businesses in Paris like Phyllis'. Her life is pretty far afield from anybody's twinkly fantasy.

Shortly after she put the first-edition Rushdie in her front window, an American tourist gestured toward the book.

"Aren't you scared?" she asked.

"Scared?" said Phyllis. "What the hell are you even talking about? This is what I do."

Phyllis Cohen's motivation for getting into the business was hardly typical, but in the 1990s and 2000s, booksellers were often called on to find their inner superhero merely to survive. Sure, the examples weren't quite as stark and violent as what Cody's had to deal with. But independent bookstore owners could not have imagined in 1990 the forces that free-market capitalism was preparing to unleash upon them, forces that would call into question ideas about books and reading that no one thought to question before: Where do you get your books? Why does it matter? What is the value of books? What exactly constitutes a book?

Despite its heroism in *The Satanic Verses* affair, Cody's Books in Berkeley was eventually one of the casualties of the digital-age shakeout in the book business, closing its doors for good in 2008. (Cody's owner Andy Ross was a good friend of Bookshop's Neal Coonerty and Coonerty played a role in convincing Ross to buy the store from its original namesake owners.) It was one of many high-profile indie bookstores in the San Francisco Bay Area to close after decades in business, including Printers Inc. in Palo Alto, Black Oak Books and Shakespeare & Co. in Berkeley and the Capitola Book Café. The book business wasn't the only sector in upheaval. The music industry, television, Hollywood and the news business were all also turned upside down and inside out. There may be no more stark generational divide in American history than between those old enough to have developed their attitudes toward art and culture in the predigital age and those who grew up with the internet and all its intended and unintended consequences. Because of the technological revolution, we've had to shoehorn into our vocabularies awkward new words for things that have existed for eons, "brick-and-mortar" bookstores and (ick!) "physical" books.

Here's where you might marshal your pro-capitalist argument. A lot of bookstores closed. So what? Maybe the market was overserved anyway. Now that Cody's is gone, is the Berkeley book lover somehow denied access to new books? Probably not. And what befalls the ground squirrel also befalls the dinosaur. Borders, the fast-growing chain that represented an existential threat to hundreds of bookstores, itself came crashing down. That's the ferment of the market. No matter how long you've been in business, you have no inherent right to market share, nor immunity from better capitalized rivals. Innovate or die. Adapt or get the hell out of the way. That's how the free market rolls, y'all.

All that makes sense. But the factor that the free market consistently fails to acknowledge is community, that fragile nexus of human connections that exists somewhere between the family and the nation-state. Community can be a neighborhood, a church, a local sports league, a service club, a nonprofit. It can also be a bookstore. When the Loma Prieta earthquake struck, Bookshop Santa Cruz was less than halfway to the fiftieth anniversary it celebrated in the fall of 2016. It was to learn pretty quickly that surviving Mother Nature was no guarantee that it would survive human nature, as reflected in the technologically evolving consumer economy. But Neal Coonerty got the message after the quake that, since the community saved Bookshop, anything he would take on to keep the bookstore solvent would not be done only on the behalf of his own livelihood. He owed the community the best fight he could give.

* * * * *

Saunter down Santa Cruz's elegant Pacific Avenue with me and let's talk about what might have been. The downtown area looks almost nothing like it did before the '89 quake. It's a lovely and inviting area, with wide sidewalks, shady benches and public art. It looks much like the tony downtown of many affluent West Coast cities, chain retailers and franchise eateries sharing space with local storekeepers and restauranteurs. Bookshop Santa Cruz isn't even the only bookstore here. Down the block is the huge used-book emporium known as Logos. Now, imagine with me, an alternative story, a moment when history could have turned, and today Santa Cruz would be synonymous with the bookselling business in a way that has nothing to do with Bookshop or any other local bookstore.

The most infamous name in bookstores around the world is that of Jeff Bezos, the founder and CEO of Amazon.com, the online retailing behemoth that is part of the Four Horsemen of the Internet Apocalypse known as "GAFA" (Google, Apple, Facebook and Amazon). Few locals realize that Santa Cruz played a crucial role in Amazon's creation story. According to Brad Stone's book *The Everything Store: Jeff Bezos and the Age of Amazon*, Bezos, then a New Yorker, visited Santa Cruz in 1994, back when morning TV talk shows were doing "What is the internet?" segments and *Wired* magazine and its many imitators were overusing the prefix "cyber."

Over blueberry pancakes at the (now defunct) Sash Mill Café, a ten-minute walk from Bookshop Santa Cruz, Bezos met with two computer programmers and pitched them a then-radical idea for an online bookstore. (Fun factoid: Amazon.com was originally to be called "Cadabra," as in the magician's hackneyed catch phrase "Abracadabra.") One of the programmers was intrigued. He was a UC Santa Cruz mathematics grad named Shel Kaphan, who had been watching a lot of hot-shot programmers flock to Netscape, the pioneering internet company in nearby Mountain View. Kaphan and Bezos were both seduced by the possibilities of the internet and the meeting went so well that, Stone's book said, the two went looking for office space in Santa Cruz.

Did they swing by Bookshop that day? Did Bezos waltz past Neal and Candy Coonerty at the front register? Did he cast an appraising eye at Bookshop's floor displays? Did he wring his hands and cackle maniacally? The best guess is no. Still, if Bezos and Kaphan were considering Santa Cruz as the birthplace of their online venture, it would have been fitting for the two men to visit the local bookstore. Ultimately, Santa Cruz lost out on a history-making opportunity (or dodged a bullet, depending on how you think about it). Bezos did the sales-tax math and figured out that it was smart business for a mail-order retailer to avoid setting up shop in a populous state like California. So it was off to Seattle.

Even if Amazon had picked Santa Cruz, it's hard to imagine that things could have been any more challenging for Bookshop's survival in the early 1990s. Neal Coonerty found himself dealing with a succession of legal hassles in the period following the earthquake. Through the Northern California Independent Booksellers Association, he had already been involved in a long legal struggle to get publishers to stop playing favorites in their discount policy to big bookstore chains. Closer to home, Bookshop was sued by the relatives of the employees killed during the earthquake in the next-door Coffee Roasting Company. That suit landed in the lap of the building's owner Ron Lau, not Neal Coonerty. A settlement was eventually reached in the case.

Once we reach the north end of Pacific Avenue, we get to the address where Bookshop stood for twenty years, the very spot where Coonerty in the days after the quake emerged from the rubble carrying his store's wooden rocking horse. Judging by what we've seen so far, you might expect to see here a wine shop, a California-chic boutique or maybe a milk bar that serves thirty-one varieties of breakfast cereal (there used to be such a thing down the block a bit). But instead, you look over and see ... nothing.

The footprint where the Bookshop building once stood is now a giant hole, surrounded by fencing. It has been ever since the building was razed after the quake. It's the last remaining evidence of the devastation of Loma Prieta, and it's been a point of consternation for city officials ever since. Locals barely notice anymore. Tourists, though, often stop and wonder why there's a cavernous hole on downtown Santa Cruz's showplace avenue, as incongruous as a missing tooth in the otherwise perfect smile of a supermodel.

On a winter's day, a little more than a year after the earthquake, the hole briefly became a stage for a beautiful and sad art installation by artist Bruce Lee and composer Jon Scoville, the first

Bookshop employee. The crater was covered by sky-blue sheets of nylon, on top of which was perched a single café table and a couple of chairs, painted white, an elegant and ghostly memorial to those who died there. Percolating up from below was a soundtrack of electronic music mixed with seabird cries, atmospheric noise and people's voices. More than twenty-five years later, the pit on Pacific remains largely unchanged, a symbol of the lingering legacy of Loma Prieta. It's also a pretty on-the-nose metaphor for the once-successful partnership between Ron Lau and Neal Coonerty.

After Bookshop had reopened in the pavilion that was renamed Booktent Santa Cruz, the expectation was that Lau's insured building would be rebuilt and that the bookstore would be back in its old site in a year or so. That first year in the Booktent, Coonerty says, business was fine. Customers were going out of their way to support the bookstore in a spirit of community support. But after a year, there had been no movement in erecting a new building and the increasing hassles of general downtown reconstruction began to take a toll on the bookstore's bottom line. "One day traffic on Cedar Street would be going in one direction," he says, "and the next day, it would be going the other way. A lot of the construction was taking out parking, and things were generally very dirty and dusty everywhere." As a practical matter, that meant it took an almost heroic effort on behalf of customers to get to the Booktent.

By the end of the second year in the Booktent, Coonerty felt trapped. At the same time, Lau was still no closer to breaking ground on a new building. Lau was busy drawing up plans that might get approval from the city and getting nowhere. He wanted to construct a beautiful new five-story building with Bookshop as its ground-level tenant. Plans for the other floors included variously, at one time or another, restaurants, apartments, an inn, a parking garage and a Japanese tea room. Finally, in November 1991, citing Lau's lack of significant progress in rebuilding, Coonerty sued, seeking to vacate the lease and move elsewhere. Lau counter-sued, blaming Coonerty for the delays. And a business relationship that began with a long-shot phone call eighteen years earlier was thus destroyed.

Coonerty wasn't willing to wait around anymore for action on what he saw as Lau's increasingly grandiose and impractical ideas. In 1992, he struck a deal to move Bookshop into a retail space in the newly reconstructed St. George Hotel. Yep, that's right: After twenty years, Bookshop Santa Cruz was moving back to its origi-nal address. This time, though, the space would be unrecognizable from the old store. The new Bookshop would have more than fifteen thousand square feet of selling space (three times the space of the prequake store), with another ten thousand square feet of storage space. The Coonertys, already dealing with legal fees and repaying FEMA loans, would have to take on some intimidating debt to make the move. They jumped at the chance anyway.

Still, Ron Lau stood in the way. In the fall of 1992, as Book-shop was making yet another call for community members to come out and help carry books to a new store, Lau sought a court injunction to stop the move, citing a "don't compete" clause in the Bookshop lease that prevented Coonerty from opening another bookstore anywhere near his building. The judge in the case de-nied the injunction saying that Coonerty would not be competing with Lau's building, given that Lau's building did not exist. The ruling did, however, keep open the possibility that Coonerty might be in violation of the lease if and when Lau opened a new building. That was a day never to come. After the Coonertys moved to the new store, Lau and the city's Redevelopment Agency could never come to an agreement on a development plan. The city, dismayed at the impasse and lamenting the eyesore of a weedy concrete hole in the ground, pressured him to sell. He refused. In 2005, the U.S. Supreme Court controversially upheld the legal basis for eminent domain, the right of governments to unilaterally take private property as long as the property owner is compensated fair market value. That same year, the Santa Cruz City Council, which by this time included Ryan Coonerty, voted unanimously to invoke eminent domain and take Ron Lau's empty lot away from him. Lau bitterly opposed the move, but within months, he finally agreed to sell the property (which wasn't the end of his legal problems, but that's for another book).

In November 1992, the Bookshop Santa Cruz Volunteer Moving and Transport Co. (a.k.a. the customers) was again mobilized to relocate Bookshop's inventory, this time from the Booktent, finally closing after three years, into the immense new space on the ground floor of the St. George. Coonerty had figured it would take a weekend. It was a heady moment, not only for the Coonertys and customers of Bookshop but for all who loved Santa Cruz. Bookshop was returning to its original address with a gorgeous new space. It was also a redemptive moment for the St. George, which had been crippled by the earthquake, then done in by a catastrophic fire a year later. What emerged was a new replica of the old hotel and with Bookshop back as its retail tenant, the 1990s were looking a lot like the 1960s, except better.

As he was making the tricky transition from the Booktent to the new Bookshop, Coonerty was entering a new phase of his life, as a politician. A lifelong liberal, Coonerty was elected to a seat on the Santa Cruz City Council in 1990. He had already served in leadership positions at the American Booksellers Association, and as vice president, he was due to step up to the position of president of the ABA when the earthquake struck. Citing his duties at home, he begged off. But moved by the response in the community to his bookstore's plight, he decided to serve in public office locally.

Santa Cruz's political history is unique enough to have served as a case study for a book on municipal politics and urban city planning, titled *The Leftmost City: Power and Progressive Politics in Santa Cruz* (Westview Press, 2008) by Richard Gendron and G. William Domhoff. The book describes a dynamic in which conservative business interests gradually and reluctantly (very reluctantly) ceded control of the city to progressives, mainly affiliated with the university. In the 1980s, those divisions were still evident on the City Council and Coonerty, who was both a downtown merchant and a progressive and supporter of the university, believed that he could serve as a bridge between the two factions.

By '92, when he was preparing to move to the St. George, Coonerty had become Santa Cruz's mayor and it was in that role that he participated in the formal unveiling of a dramatic new downtown the following year. Bookshop had a dazzling new space, and a nine-screen cinema was being built on the next block. Other displaced businesses, most notably the used-book emporium Logos, were also reopening in spacious new buildings. The Dionysian old Pacific Garden Mall was forever gone, to be replaced by a more Apollonian Pacific Avenue. The transformation from one to the other had been trying for everyone, none more so than the merchants. At one point, with the streets and sidewalks still under construction, downtown visitors were forced to walk a maze of plywood passageways between businesses and the clomping around sounded like something you would hear in a cowboy town from an old Hollywood movie.

In 1993, however, the downtown was finally liberated from the dirt, noise and limited mobility of construction. A sense of newness and possibility pervaded the city. People were elated. In Bookshop's narrative, these were the good old days. The earthquake, the tents, the battle with Lau, all that was in the rear view. For months, Bookshop welcomed wide-eyed customers visiting the huge new space for the first time. Life was good.

CHAPTER 10

Waiting for a Sign

If you were alive and ambulatory in the 1990s, you probably stumbled into a Super Crown Books store once or twice, if for no other reason than to ask about a bathroom. Super Crown was a discount retailer, which meant in designing a convivial and welcoming atmosphere, they probably hired the same guy that the Foot Locker used. If given a choice, bookstore snobs would mostly prefer walking barefoot in a Filipino fish market than visiting a Super Crown. In Santa Cruz, the store was spacious but aggressively uninteresting. You'd be greeted by big, half-hearted displays of generic bestsellers, cookbooks with lots of color pictures but no soul, celebrity memoirs that had been semi-hot for two weeks three years before, and some repackaged public-domain titles in case you had recently lost your faux-leather-bound copy of *Treasure Island*. Picture the book tables at Costco, except not as classy. The signage reminded browsers of the discounts that awaited them at checkout and instead of the buzz of ambient chatter, you usually got the pervasive, carpet-muffled quiet of a shopping mall department store in the first minutes after opening. By contrast, in its new store just across the street from Super Crown, Bookshop Santa Cruz was working to curate its shopping experience to reflect what the local community knew and loved. Neal or Candy Coonerty hovered by the front register, often chatting with friends and customers, gesturing warily over their shoulder at the new store in town. In a routine that would be repeated for years, customers in line to buy *The Celestine Prophecy* or the latest Anne Rice novel would declare to the clerk in a kind of performative over-loud voice that they were supporting Bookshop and would never think of even visiting that other store.

If Neal Coonerty believed that having survived a catastrophic earthquake he could endure anything fate would throw his way, Super Crown was the first test of that attitude. Super Crown was a spinoff of Crown Books, a retailer that began in 1977 in the Washington, D.C., area and, within fifteen years, had grown to be one of the largest bookstore chains in the country. Super Crown's emphasis was on discounting, a strategy that undermined the business model for independent bookstores everywhere. This practice was at the heart of the long dispute between indie booksellers and the chains in which Coonerty was a central player at the American Booksellers Association.

In the fall of 1995, Super Crown opened a big new store on Pacific Avenue, less than a hundred steps from Bookshop's front entrance. The new store was offering bestsellers and many other titles at big discounts, up to forty percent. To match those discounts, Bookshop would have had to sacrifice its entire profit margin. Super Crown was Exhibit A in the ABA's beef with publishers who were giving discounts to chains that they weren't offering to indies. Coonerty believed that the chain opening a block away from his store was not a coincidence, that Crown wanted to shut him down.

Coonerty was aggressive against Super Crown from the beginning. On the day before Super Crown opened for business in Santa Cruz, he was already telling everyone who would listen that a big fight was brewing between the two booksellers. "Your worst competitor is a stupid competitor," Coonerty told interviewer Irene Reti for a University of California oral history of Bookshop Santa Cruz. By that, he meant that the price breaks that Super Crown and other chains were offering were not sustainable, that the book business just didn't have the profit margins to survive that kind of deep discounting. He felt that Crown was playing a game of chicken with its competitors, which included Barnes & Noble and Borders. The way Coonerty saw it, Super Crown and Bookshop were hanging by the same rope and Crown was willing to cut the rope, confident that it would survive the fall and Bookshop would not. Considering the earthquake debt and legal bills Bookshop was facing, the strategy made a certain amount of sense, in the same way that kamikaze attacks make sense.

Instead of waiting to be smothered by Crown's price advantage, Coonerty jumped out ready to land the first punch. If he was waiting for a sign of what to do, Crown provided it. Shortly before it opened, Super Crown went to the city and asked for a variance on an ordinance regarding the size of exterior signage. Crown wanted a sign for its store that was bigger than the ordinance stipulated. "They were asking for favors," says Coonerty. "We were looking for a fight in order to define for the town that it was us versus them, and this was it." The vote went against him and Crown got its big, brightly lit sign. "To tell you the truth," he says, "that was fine by us. It wasn't about the sign. It was about framing the debate. And, generally, I think it worked. We were able to say, this is an outside corporation coming in here asking for special favors. Bookshop had to obey the sign ordinance. Why didn't they?" Later, Coonerty claimed that a lawyer from Crown called him, enraged by the sign controversy, and threatened to squash Bookshop "like an ant."

Support for Coonerty in his battle against Super Crown was, however, pretty far from unanimous. A significant number of Santa Cruzans were hostile to Bookshop's David vs. Goliath crusade. Many saw arrogance in Coonerty's insistence that consumers pay higher prices just for the privilege of having Bookshop Santa Cruz around. They saw a distasteful exploitation of political muscle exerted for the sake of a private business (even though the council voted against Coonerty). And they framed the issue as a matter of freedom of choice for consumers. Who was this guy to deny me a better price if the free market could provide it?

Coonerty was caricatured by both sides. He was either the plucky, defiant little guy standing up to the ruthless and homogenizing corporate chains. Or he was the hairy left-leaning commie inserting himself between you and your freedom to buy a cheaper book. Either way, it didn't matter too much. After only three years in business, Santa Cruz's Super Crown closed its doors for good in 1998, falling victim to an almost Shakespearean personal drama between the corporation's founder and his family. The family feud hurled Crown into financial trouble and within a couple of years the company was in bankruptcy.

If Coonerty's history with Bookshop was a series of picking fights against bullies, some of those fights were playful. In the 1990s, bloviating radio host Rush Limbaugh afflicted liberals for three hours a day with mocking invective against Democratic politicians, activists, feminists and others. When Limbaugh's collection of rhetorical fire bombs called *See, I Told You So* was released, Coonerty decided to have some fun with the old blowhard.

It was never Coonerty's style to refuse to sell a book for political reasons, no matter how odious he found its contents. When Bret Easton Ellis's luridly violent *American Psycho* was released, Coonerty displayed it with a sign that read: "We believe this book has a right to be published, but we cannot recommend it." With the book *The Bell Curve,* which argued that there were differences in intelligence among the races, Coonerty displayed it surrounded by other titles that refuted its thesis. As a bookseller and as a prominent member of the independent booksellers' trade organization, he felt that he had to stand up for the First Amendment every time. "Everybody buying a murder mystery isn't planning a murder," he says. "Someone buying *Mein Kampf* isn't necessarily a Nazi. We don't know why people buy stuff. Our job is to carry it."

In the case of Rush, he decided to sell the book at the price per pound of bologna, hearkening back to his stunt with Richard Nixon's memoir twenty years earlier. Proceeds from all sales of the book were to go to causes Limbaugh would find odious, namely the Santa Cruz AIDS Project and the National Organization for Women.

This time, though, the target of Coonerty's gag responded. Limbaugh caught wind of the promotion and blasted Coonerty on his radio show, laughing at the foolishness of Coonerty selling the book at a loss. Limbaugh's "dittoheads" responded by flooding Bookshop with orders, to hurt Coonerty in the wallet. One guy tried to order a thousand copies to which a quick-thinking Coonerty added a ten-dollar service charge per book.

It wasn't the first time that Limbaugh had tangled with Santa Cruz, or Coonerty. The year before, the City Council passed an ordinance, sponsored by Coonerty, that would bar discrimination in employment or housing based on personal appearance. The so-called "looks law" was an effort to protect transsexuals while still allowing employers to have dress codes and cleanliness standards. Conservatives and Limbaugh caricatured the ordinance as a means for liberals to force private employers to hire people with studs in their tongues and bones in their noses. Opponents called it the "ugly ordinance." Limbaugh waved it around as more proof that Santa Cruz had become a haven for "liberal wackos."

"People were leaving Bibles on our doorstep," remembered Ryan Coonerty, a teenager at the time. Several months before, Ryan himself drew the ire of Limbaugh with a stunt that had nothing to do with his dad. Ryan had already suffered because of his dad's political stances. Playing on the school football team while your dad was fighting for transgender rights wasn't a particularly comfortable position to be in in 1991. But the son had inherited some of the mischievous spirit of the father. As the editor of the Santa Cruz High School newspaper, Ryan Connerty reacted to the news that basketball star Magic Johnson had AIDS by deciding to put a free condom inside every copy of his paper, sparking another community tempest that eventually found its way to Limbaugh's office.

Candy Coonerty was not happy that her seventeen-year-old son was suddenly the condom king of Santa Cruz and drawing fire from Rush Limbaugh. The incident, says Ryan, caused some angst in the household. Dad, however, just gave a wink, cracking that he was proud that Ryan taped the condoms into the newspapers instead of stapling them. "It was super fun," says Ryan. "But overall, it was a realization: With a little bit of effort, a little bit of willingness to put your neck out and a little creativity to get some attention, you could drive a national conversation."

In the years to come, Neal Coonerty would return to the snarky publicity stunt to get attention for Bookshop. He sold one of Newt Gingrich's many political books with a barf bag and a plea to readers to resist sending a used bag to Gingrich, all the while providing the House Speaker's Washington address. Later, borrowing an idea from Austin, Texas, Coonerty printed up bumper stickers with the phrase "Keep Santa Cruz Weird." Again, Coonerty's aim was only to celebrate the eccentricities of Santa Cruz, and again his enemies willfully misunderstood him. "It was meant to be about the street performers, not the street people," he says. "Funny, everybody out of town got it. But in Santa Cruz, people took it in a very negative way, as if I were supporting syringes being left on the sidewalks all over town."

As the new millennium approached, things were looking good at Bookshop Santa Cruz. Super Crown had collapsed and somehow, against all odds, Bookshop was still clinging to the rope. Neal had found his post-earthquake equilibrium, and he was having fun. Yet if there is anything to that old cliché "It's always darkest just before the dawn," then the opposite must also be true occasionally. Sometimes, the sun comes out just before the terrible storm.

CHAPTER 11

'A Second Earthquake'

The Jewish cemetery in Santa Cruz sneaks up on you. One minute, you're walking along a gently sloping street through a serene, affluent neighborhood past a wide, inviting greenway. Then, you encounter an unmarked but unmistakable kind of boundary, beyond which is a noticeably different terrain. On your right, next to a vast grassy upward-rising meadow is a severe multistory clapboard farmhouse, the kind you might find in a Laura Ingalls Wilder novel or some place on the Montana frontier that Bonnie and Clyde might have used as a hideout.

Across the street from that house is the cemetery, situated in a thick grove of eucalyptus and Monterey cypress. On some mornings in the late summer, the coastal fog seems to hang on here a bit longer than in the neighborhood nearby, as if the treetops were clinging to it.

On the front gate is a small sign reminding visitors that Jewish law forbids "any living soul" inside the cemetery on Shabbat, from sundown Friday to sundown Saturday. At any other time, you're welcome to visit and pay your respects to the one hundred eighty-plus souls buried here. The oldest graves, toward the back of the grove just before the thickets of poison oak that slope into a deep canyon, date back to the 1870s, which is ancient by California standards. It's among the more recent graves, in a shady spot closer to the road, where you'll find Candy Issenman Coonerty.

Candy's grave lies beside that of her mother, Ruth. There was a day sometime in the distant past when neither woman could have guessed that their ultimate resting places would be in a California surf town. They were, after all, from Montreal, a European-tinted river city of wrought iron and harsh winters. But they were delivered here by a web of circumstances that could never be replicated and by people who were doing not much more than following hunches: Candy's brother giving her a poster on which was advertised a literary conference in Ireland; Neal Coonerty, stumbling in on the same conference; that unknown person who cancelled their reservation at the last minute allowing Neal to attend; years later, Ron Lau, deciding to sell both his business and his house to the Coonertys. The cards fell, the dominoes toppled, all the roads not taken leading to a million elsewheres.

Candy's parents followed her and Neal to Santa Cruz, first to visit, then to live. Neal remembers that first time he brought his in-laws to Santa Cruz, while he was still negotiating to get the bookstore. "It was the July Fourth weekend, and we got stuck in traffic on Ocean Street, surrounded by all these intimidating-looking bikers on motorcycles and I could see Candy's mother thinking, 'This is where my daughter is going to live?'"

Candy died on July 22, 1999, a few months short of her fiftieth birthday. She had been living with lupus, a chronic auto-immune disease, often hard to diagnose. In the early '90s, she suffered a stroke, brought on by a cerebral hemorrhage. At the time, she was attending a bar mitzvah and called Casey, then only seventeen, slurring into the phone, "I can't speak and I can't walk. Please help me." Both Neal and Ryan were out of town. Casey got her mom to the hospital and stayed with her until her father and brother arrived. "The hardest thing I had ever done was not to cry," Casey wrote later in an essay about that painful period. "I had to hold it all inside to protect her from my fear."

Candy recovered from that stroke, but several years later, in the spring of 1999, she was struck with a much more serious one. She was at her favorite salon when it happened. "While she was getting her hair washed, she began to feel weird," says Neal. "They called the ambulance, and by that night, she was already in a vegetative state." Seven weeks later, she slipped away and was buried among the eucalyptus.

Today, Candy's spirit is still present at Bookshop Santa Cruz, in a small memorial shrine in the cards and gifts section, which she curated for years. There's a photo of her, a chain of paper cranes created in her memory by Bookshop's employees shortly after her death, and an old weathered memorial book, full of signatures and painfully articulated thoughts from friends and customers – "A second earthquake shakes Bookshop," "Bookshelves around the world are stacked with memories of you."

Her husband had always been the public face of Bookshop Santa Cruz and after he was elected to the City Council and then mayor, Neal's public image broke the bounds of Bookshop, becoming the dominant image of liberal Santa Cruz. It was always Candy, though, who excelled at the person-to-person relationships with customers, with distributers and suppliers, with employees. She had wider experiences in the business outside Santa Cruz than Neal did. She managed Bookshop's satellite store Bookworks in Aptos. After that, she was the bookstore's buyer for cards, calendars, journals and gifts. She even worked for a while outside Bookshop as a sales rep for a greeting card company.

"Before the earthquake," says Ryan, "she was very much involved in the store, but I don't think it was central to who she was. After the earthquake, it was different. She really saw it as her store. My dad was upstairs in his office and she was down on the floor every day, dealing with the employees, catching the shoplifters. She was much more the social piece of it. Even today, people come up to me and say, 'Oh, I remember your mom always greeting me when I walked in the door.' She was the personality of the store, the real heart of it."

In his eulogy for Candy, Neal said, "I was the public face that people associated with our work and our lives, but Candy was the hard labor and spirit making it happen. While our roles seemed clear to the public, the reality was different. She saw our dreams and made them come true. She believed in me, and made me believe."

She served as a vital counterbalance to her husband's business instincts. He was a risk-taker. She defaulted to caution. He saw the value of publicity. She preferred to stay behind the scenes. He was a big-picture thinker. She focused on the day-to-day. He enjoyed engaging opponents in the political arena. She was not always comfortable with his political life. She was devoted to the faith of her Jewish forebears in a way that Neal was not to his Catholic ones. She was a central figure in the local synagogue, raising her two children as practicing Jews.

Again and again, she filled in the spaces, allowing Neal to be Neal, earning respect for her down-to-earth approach from just about anyone she encountered. "Agewise, she was my junior," says Bookshop manager Patrick O'Connell, "but maturity-wise, she was always my senior."

Yet, people are complex. They are rarely one thing or another. It has become part of Bookshop mythology that Candy was always cautious where Neal was bold. But she steadfastly supported him, even in many of his bigger risks. And considering that she was once a Quebec girl with a degree from Emerson College who threw her lot in with a shaggy Berkeley hippie and fled to California to chase some unlikely dream, it's clear that there was a rebel heart inside Candy Issenman after all.

At the end of his eulogy, Neal decided to read a poem he had written for Candy, from the period before they were married and both still in college on opposite sides of the country. The poem, he said, was never meant for anyone's eyes but hers. Throughout their life together, it hung framed on the wall of their bedroom. It ended with this: "When the wind melts into the blue of the sky/ your shadows will wander like small animals/ seeking shelter and here they will find my eyes."

CHAPTER 12

A Body Blow

There was a time, back in the 1990s, when I thrilled at the sight of a Borders or a Barnes & Noble. For me, it was the era of family traveling, the kind of archetypal road trips you're supposed to do before your kids reach the age when they are disgusted at the sight of you. When my wife, my two young daughters and I would take off into the Western interior, we'd often find a Borders or Barnes & Noble in which we could dependably burn two or three hours, each of us sealed off in our own little media-dense bubble, before we hit the road again. We used these big-box bookstores in the same way we used Trader Joe's or Panera Bread, as acceptable touchstones while away from the familiarities of home. Like most West Coasters, we were all a little wary of what we might find in America beyond the fog belt and we embraced a few chain retailers on the road that we might never have patronized at home. After one particularly media-less (and, as a consequence, gloriously relaxing) week at a remote cabin near Lake Tahoe, we jumped in the car and drove to Reno where we gratefully found a Borders, stumbled into it like bewildered desert wanderers into Babylon and wasted an entire afternoon in the place. My oldest girl hung out at the listening stations in the music section. My youngest dragged out the picture books. The wife copied down home improvement ideas from the gardening section and I plugged in my laptop to catch up on the news while slurping down the best coffee I'd had all week. At that moment, I loved Borders for reminding us what civilization felt like.

Throughout the 1990s and 2000s, Borders was a bookselling juggernaut. At its most powerful, it had more than twelve hundred stores around the world. Borders was part of the Big Box Era, when many successful retailers were dramatically scaling up from successful local or regional businesses, eventually morphing into too-familiar brand-name franchises that were turning every town and suburb in America into Anywhere, USA. Just as Starbucks spread out from Seattle and Whole Foods metastasized from Austin, Borders was once a single store in Ann Arbor, Michigan, founded by two brothers who were students at the University of Michigan.

In '99, Borders had its eye on the Santa Cruz County market and first expressed interest in a proposed development at a sweet spot just off the freeway in Santa Cruz's picturesque neighbor city Capitola. This was extremely bad news for the nearby Capitola Book Café and opposition to the proposed deal quickly blossomed. Fans of the Book Café mobilized and petitioned the Capitola City Council to quash the plan. Among those who spoke before the City Council on behalf of the Book Café was Neal Coonerty who, as part of the American Booksellers Association's suits against publishers, had crossed swords with Borders before.

The Capitola City Council attempted to cut the baby in half by approving the deal, but only for half the square footage that

Borders had requested, on the grounds that such superstores were out of character to the quaint coastal village vibe that the city had worked to cultivate for years. One local woman commented that she didn't want to live in "San Jose-by-the-Sea." History doesn't record representatives from Borders rolling their eyes and muttering "You gotta be f*$%# kidding me," but the upshot is that Borders walked away from the deal. And that was that. Or so everyone thought.

A couple of months later, as if to say "You want hardball? Fine, let's play hardball," Borders announced its plan to move into a roomy new space in the heart of Santa Cruz's downtown, a pleasant five-minute stroll from the front door of Bookshop Santa Cruz.

The timing of the news about Borders, coming just two months after Candy's death, could not have been worse. Considering that Bookshop was a tangible symbol of the Coonertys' marriage, that it was as much Candy's store as his own, given that he was at that time the president of the American Booksellers Association which for years had been slugging it out for the sake of fairness to little-guy independents, and had sued Borders under federal antitrust laws for monopolistic practices, Coonerty felt he had no choice but to fight the Borders opening as hard as he could fight it.

"It was a body blow," says Ryan Coonerty. "It took a hard time and made it harder."

Neal soon found himself dealing with the kind of anger you can only get to through grief. It wasn't only anger at a big-box behemoth engaging in what he was convinced were predatory, zero-sum business practices, but anger at the cosmos, at fate, at the cruel and abrupt dictates of death.

"Candy had died," says Neal. "Something inside her had killed her. There was no fight against that. I couldn't do anything about it. I felt really helpless. Well, I was not going to be helpless watching my business go down."

In the months that followed, the debate on whether Borders moving into Santa Cruz was a good thing or a bad thing spread from Bookshop to the local news media to the City Council to the kitchens and patios of nearly everyone with a stake in downtown. From one perspective, this was a case of an outside corporation muscling in on a community it knew nothing about and threatening a beloved local business that was serving its clientele just fine. From the other perspective, here was a downtown merchant using his political connections to protect his own livelihood at the expense of consumers and freedom of choice.

"My dad was so angry," says Ryan. "He focused his grief and anger on this issue. Everything was so raw. The debate was so excruciating. It just caused this issue to escalate to really personal levels. I mean, if it had been two years earlier, it would have been dealt with differently, with marketing and humor. But this was a straight-out brawl."

Many in city government stood with Bookshop, announcing that Borders was not welcome in Santa Cruz, accusing the chain of being predatory. Despite that support, in a dramatic vote in November, the City Council voted five to two in favor of granting Borders a permit to open. One councilman who voted with the majority said that his decision "made me sick to my stomach."

The Borders fight was fundamentally different than the Super Crown fight. Super Crown was not a store that had a lot of customer goodwill behind it, despite its discount prices. By contrast, Borders came to town with a good reputation, at least among consumers. Even indie booksellers praised Borders for bringing books to regions that otherwise didn't have bookstores. Borders was itself once an indie bookstore, and even as it scaled up dramatically, it was able to internalize the values of an indie bookstore – wide selections of genres and titles, adjacent cafes, comfortable chairs that encouraged loitering. They even offered music and DVDs. "They were a great store," says Neal Coonerty. "Super Crown was one-dimensional. Those people didn't know books. But Borders was a good operation."

In the first week of June 2000, Borders opened its doors in downtown Santa Cruz, amidst waves of anticipation and dread. Some of the Coonertys' activist allies didn't do them any favors. The new store was subject to graffiti and other vandalism. It claimed to be the victim of stink bomb attacks. Someone opened a fire valve in the building and sent thousands of gallons of water flooding into the store. The store's manager was pelted with rocks. People picketed outside Borders singing songs such as "The United States of Generica." Still, customers defiantly visited the store, some engaging the protesters in heated debate about their freedom to shop wherever they wanted to shop. One Borders customer was caught on camera telling protesters to "Go to hell, communists."

These kinds of confrontations only served to make Neal Coonerty's life more miserable. He deplored vandalism and bullying and he was savvy enough to know that such things were much more damaging to Bookshop than helpful. He went before television cameras to denounce the vandalism and the aggressive protests, but he still caught hell from the editorial page of the *Santa Cruz Sentinel* and in other forums from people who insisted that his anti-corporate rhetoric was to blame for turning book shopping into a political donnybrook. If you saw Coonerty on television during that time, looking ashen and exhausted, it's easy to imagine that the Irish love of the political fight that had buoyed him in the decade after the earthquake had all but evaporated. What was left was a man still grieving his wife, sensing that the business he built with her by his side was moving closer every day to being bulldozed by an enormous and relentless competitor. And somehow, perversely, he was coming across as the bad guy.

Richard Lange, one of the handful of people who have worked

as booksellers for both the Capitola Book Café and Bookshop, told me, "There's always been part of the community of Santa Cruz that resents Santa Cruz. By that I mean the liberalism, Pacific Avenue, the whole progressive vibe, and Neal was the name and face of what they resented." That sector of the community, says Lange, saw Borders as a kind of white knight. "It was their time to come out and gloat, to go to that store to spite Neal Coonerty."

Still, Coonerty was far from alone. He heard from plenty of loyal customers who daily let him and the staff know that their book-buying dollars were staying with Bookshop. In the first year or two after Borders opened, going to Bookshop was akin to walking into Cheers. Maybe not everybody knew your name, but you were bound to see someone familiar, browsing the shelves mostly to be seen as a loyal soldier for the Bookshop cause. The subject of Borders was never very far from any conversation.

Down the block, Borders was attracting crowds as well. Like many of its stores, the Santa Cruz Borders was a show palace of media products, with an upstairs café that invited lingering. The turn of the millennium was a boom time for Borders as it profited from several concurrent phenomena: the Harry Potter frenzy began bringing kids and families into bookstores in the late 1990s, the film industry conversion from VHS to DVD made movie collecting popular again and the development of Wi-Fi technology transformed cafés and coffeehouses into hangouts.

Back in Santa Cruz, though, walking into Borders might cost you social capital. Lee Quarnstrom, a columnist for the *San Jose Mercury News*, had a second-floor office right across the street from Borders. As a joke, he would sometimes call Coonerty to report on who he saw go in and out of Borders. People carrying Borders shopping bags were unwittingly the target of oh-so-subtle sneers, and there could be no greater social gaffe than to walk into Bookshop Santa Cruz with a Borders bag. You'd feel more welcome if you walked in wearing no pants.

A reporter friend of mine told me he once spied Coonerty late one night peering into the window at Borders. Neal himself says that he went inside the Borders store in Santa Cruz only once. After hearing that a Borders store at the World Trade Center was destroyed in the 9/11 terrorist attacks, Coonerty delivered a card and a bouquet of flowers in sympathy and solidarity to the Santa Cruz store. The manager at the Borders, he reported, was grateful and quite gracious.

Still, Borders put a serious hurt on Bookshop's bottom line. The pain was first felt on two specific demographics: summertime tourists and UC Santa Cruz students. In both instances, it was a case of people from out of town opting for Borders because it was familiar to them. Neither tourists nor students were too tuned in to shop-local movements, and neither cared a whole lot about Bookshop's history as a symbol of downtown Santa Cruz.

These were not happy days at Bookshop, and Borders wasn't solely to blame. A confluence of factors dramatically eroded Bookshop's profitability. This was the era of the Dot Com Bust, the painful market correction following years of wild Wall Street speculation when the promise of the World Wide Web seemed limitless. (The easiest way to be pelted with bags full of money in those days was to say the word "startup" in front of the right crowd. How else to explain "Pets.com"?) When the snapback came, it was particularly rough on Bay Area companies, including those in Santa Cruz.

It was also the time when the icy fingers of Amazon began to curl around the neck of the bookstore industry. Bookstore employees from the period (from Bookshop, Capitola Book Café, even Borders) all seem to have anecdotes of customers copying down titles in the store that they would then order from Amazon when they got home. Simple morality didn't always translate to the act of buying books in those days. Booksellers were regularly flummoxed by those customers who would merrily admit to this practice, as if telling a bookstore clerk that you were going to spend your dollar at Amazon was as value neutral as telling them you're going to stop and get an ice cream across the street.

Taken together, Borders, the Dot Com Bust and the rise of Amazon was a disaster for booksellers nationwide, and Bookshop was no different. "Because of the grief and loss we had suffered," Casey Coonerty Protti says, "it took us a couple of years to really respond to Borders. And we got into a hole because of it." Even before Borders opened, Neal was still dealing with debt from the earthquake. When sales took a deep dive in the early 2000s, he had to take out loans on his house – his and Candy's house, the house where they raised their children – to keep the business open.

CHAPTER 13

'Is It 2009 Yet?

Neal and Candy's two children both turned out to be high achievers. Ryan, now a writer, teacher and entrepreneur, graduated from the University of Oregon and earned a master's at the London School of Economics and a law degree from the University of Virginia. Casey, like her dad, went to UC Berkeley and from there received her MBA at Northwestern and then a master's at the John F. Kennedy School of Government at Harvard. Inheriting Bookshop was not necessarily a part of the plan for either Ryan or Casey.

Both say that throughout their upbringing, their parents never pressured them to follow in their footsteps. They never encouraged the kids to think about taking over the bookstore one day or discouraged them. The truth was, they were ambivalent. "My parents were just as scared of us doing it as they were excited for us doing it," Casey says. There was never an overt expectation, but both always knew there was a chance the bookstore's fate would ultimately fall to either or both of them.

Eventually, a choice had to be made. Ryan spent his youth working summers at Bookshop, owing, he says, to his "strong back and weak mind." Neal laid the cards on the table at the appropriate time, but was still wary of pushing. "He told us, 'You have x number of years to decide whether you want to be in the business or not. At some point, you have to be able to make the decision. If you don't want to do it, that's OK. We'll figure out something else.'"

Neither Ryan nor Casey had any illusions about how difficult diving into the book business would be. Neither could be lulled into a fantasy that owning a bookstore was mostly about opening boxes of new books, chatting with brilliant authors and pondering Proust all day. "It's almost none of that," says Ryan. "It's figuring out the plumbing and scheduling problems and accounting issues and health-care issues." Ryan Coonerty was destined to go on and wrestle with those problems as cofounder of NextSpace, a company that gave freelancers, entrepreneurs and telecommuters an urban office space environment, and an excuse to wear something besides pajamas all day. By 2016, NextSpace had eight locations, seven of which were in California. Ryan did, however, follow in the footsteps of his dad in the political realm. He went on to serve on the Santa Cruz City Council and as the city's mayor. In the late 2000s, Neal took on the job of Santa Cruz County supervisor, and after his retirement, Ryan was elected and moved into the same office, both politically and literally. "They didn't even have to change the name plate," Ryan says, standing in the same office that his father occupied.

Casey Coonerty Protti also took over an office vacated by her father, this one overlooking the sales floor at Bookshop Santa Cruz. She knew that if she did not take the reins, Neal would be forced into selling. She grabbed the opportunity, but out of more than family obligation. "It was really what I wanted to do," she says. In grad school, she had studied public policy with an idea of working in mission-based nonprofit management. Then, it struck her: "This business is as mission-based as any nonprofit." The family connections, carrying the Coonerty name in Santa Cruz with all its positive (and otherwise) effects, all that was a bonus. What may have cinched it was the memory of her mother. "I feel closer to her here than anywhere else," Casey says.

In 2006, it became official. Neal Coonerty, who was already running for county supervisor, was retiring as the owner and operator of Bookshop Santa Cruz. Casey Coonerty Protti, who had grown up in the store, who had ridden the store's hobby horse as a toddler, was taking over. It was a gratifying moment for Neal. "She's smarter than I am," he says. "She's better trained academically than I was, and she had more energy. Over the years, I had seen people running their businesses get tired of it, or get distracted by something else, and they didn't do a good job. I recognized that I was getting tired."

Once Neal stepped away, he allowed Casey the room to run things as she saw fit. They would continue to have lunch together regularly, but from that moment, "she's been 99 percent running the store." Neal kept his hand in Bookshop by taking a shift at the cash register once a week. Ten years later, long retired from his county supe job, he was still showing up for work every Friday morning.

Casey had little time to celebrate the inauguration of a new era at Bookshop. The store was teetering on the verge of collapse. She was only thirty. Two months into her tenure, she found out she was pregnant. Fighting Amazon and Borders felt more and more like a two-front war that Bookshop was losing. The burst of the internet bubble at the end of the '90s was painful enough, but just as the local economy was crawling out of that, a much more serious economic catastrophe loomed with the Wall Street crisis of 2008.

On top of all that, the rise of e-books represented a new worry, threatening to separate readers from bookstores, and brought forth a lot of weird new existential questions about the business that Casey's parents never had to face: Is reading on a screen going to replace reading on paper? Are we about to enter a post-book period? What is a "book," anyway?

Casey was much more hands-on than her dad was. She relied on the loyalty of her customer base, many of whom were paying attention and were beginning to grasp the unique squeeze that Bookshop was feeling, but at at the same time she made changes, cutbacks, decisions on automation and monetization, all those things that were abstractions back in grad school. She combed over every line item in her budget. She allowed attrition to reduce her staff and trained her staffers to be more versatile in covering customers' needs. She tried to meet the e-books challenge by urging readers to buy them through Bookshop. She also offered e-readers for sale. It was a tough, frustrating time, made all the more scary by the cascade of "Print Is Dead!" articles circulating online.

And yes, sometimes a business just gets lucky. Sometimes a crazy idea turns into something that sounds not so crazy in retrospect. Shortly after President George W. Bush's re-election in 2004, bumper stickers started cropping up in liberal pockets of the country, especially Santa Cruz, reading "Is it 2009 yet?" In the grand tradition of the impish political stunts of his past, Neal Coonerty tuned in to his inner Mort Sahl to scare up a bit more revenue for the store. He dreamed up the Bush Countdown Clock, the bastard brainchild of Limbaugh-for-the-price-of-bologna and the Gingrich barf bags. He ordered a bunch of electronic gizmos, flat, about the size of a credit card that you could use as a key chain. The thing would count down the minutes, hours and days until Bush was finally out of office. He slapped a picture of Dubya on his gizmo, calibrated it to Inauguration Day 2009, and the Bush Countdown

Clock was born.

It was prominently displayed by the front register of Bookshop. And it sold like cold beer on a hot day. A website was set up to sell the countdown clocks to a wider international audience. Before long, Bookshop was selling them wholesale to other booksellers from Coonerty's long contact list from his days at the American Booksellers Association. Media in the U.S. and Canada were picking up on the story. The markup was healthy, much more so than on any book in the store, and they sold tens of thousands. "The money we made on the Bush Countdown Clock really saved the Bookshop," says Neal.

Without the Bush Countdown Clock, given the jarring and painful recession ushered in by the Wall Street meltdown, Bookshop Santa Cruz may have faced the kind of awkward, drawn-out end game that eventually took down its friendly rival the Capitola Book Café. Casey admitted that she lacks the gene for bold gambits that Neal possessed. "I'm much more risk averse than my dad or my brother, especially with the kind of thing that would splash across the front page in a political way," she says. "I'm more the one who would say, 'Hmmm, let's talk about this.' But at the end of the day, this was just fun. It made people laugh when they really needed a laugh."

George W. Bush really did leave office in 2009 (you can look it up), and Barack Obama, a black man with an African name, became his replacement, bedazzling liberals and appalling conservatives. That miracle had a negligible effect on Bookshop's bottom line. But another surprise that came along a couple of years later was a godsend. In early 2011, Borders Books & Music declared Chapter 11 bankruptcy and announced that it was closing two hundred stores, including the twenty-two thousand square foot Xanadu in downtown Santa Cruz.

It is unseemly to celebrate the failure of a business. In Santa Cruz, at least thirty people lost their jobs. Yet, for the partisans of Bookshop Santa Cruz (not to mention Logos Books, Streetlight

Records and other local businesses that had felt the squeeze from Borders), that day in 2011 felt like a victory.

Casey Protti and her family were on vacation in Hawaii when the word came down. She had heard beforehand that Borders was planning on making an announcement, possibly of store closures. She was up at five in the morning in Hawaii, on speaker phone with her floor staff back in Santa Cruz. Her husband, Michel, who at the time worked at Yahoo, had found the five-page document that Borders had released on the internet, listing the closures. Michel was scanning every page in real time while the Bookshop staff held its collective breath back in California. Then, on the last page, there it was: Santa Cruz was among the stores to be closed. "I didn't quite believe it," says Casey. "I wanted seven different confirmations to know that it was true." But there it was, in black and white. Casey blurted the news over speaker phone. Everybody started screaming. Then came the crying.

Casey drafted a letter to her customers on the Borders closing. She answered phone calls from reporters wanting comment. Later, at some point, she called her dad, the former bookseller now working as a county supervisor. Neal was pleased, says Casey, but in a distinctly "I knew it would all work out" kind of way. "He's the eternal optimist," she says. "He always thought the best thing was going to happen. And I was the opposite, having convinced myself that I had to plan my whole life around the fact that Borders was never going to go away."

By the time she had returned to the mainland from Hawaii, having made time on vacation to confer with the Bookshop staff about next steps, she had decided to offer some kind of outreach for the laid-off employees at Borders. Driving home from the airport, Casey made her husband drive past Borders, where she saw giant "Going Out of Business" signs hanging in every window. She took photos. Only then was it real.

CHAPTER 14

'A Fighting Chance'

Indie bookstores aren't only good for the communities they serve. They're good for readers and writers. Big chains have a homogenizing effect. To the degree that we're all eating takeout Chipotle's burritos and drinking Blue Moon beer at a table we bought in a box at Ikea, that's bad for the small taqueria, the neighborhood microbrewery and the artisan furniture maker. A book, though, is a creature of a different order from a table. It is a vessel of ideas, and when ideas are homogenous, cultures wither and die. Without indie bookstores, the publishing industry would be in danger of losing its great middle, what used to be called the "midlist," those authors who aren't the superstars but who make a workman-type living catering to a loyal audience.

"In a place like Bookshop," says novelist Jonathan Franzen, "you have employees reading a lot of galleys and deciding among themselves what is going to appeal to the local community. Because it's not a top-down structure, but more of a bottom-up structure, you get more idiosyncratic choices. Because you have a lot of indie bookstores operating in the same way, it really helps with those second-level books, books that are worthy but that aren't going to be bought in huge numbers. Those books now have a fighting chance because you have a dozen employees at a hundred different independent bookstores, sifting through and looking for something that's very good."

Much like movie studios chasing after the next superhero franchise, big publishers increasingly focus their energies on the Big Book, laying bets on the next *Gone Girl* or *The Goldfinch*. Chain bookstores are like the giant mall multiplexes playing *Batman v Superman* on three screens. Indie bookstores not only reflect their communities more fully, they reflect the interests of the people they hire. Bookshop Santa Cruz has developed a towering reputation for instilling the love of reading in kids, thanks largely to Gä Lombard, the store's longtime children's book buyer. Gä (pronounced *gay*) presides over a magic fiefdom of children's books in a section that accounts for about a quarter of Bookshop's entire retail floor space and about a quarter of its sales receipts.

"All my friends who have kids, at some point I bring them in contact with Gä," says bestselling author Laurie R. King. "She knows how to get information out of kids. You see an adolescent shrug when you ask them about what they like. Gä manages to direct that shrug and find out what they like underneath, which means she can put two or three books in the kid's hands that they'll enjoy. It's like going to a first-rate therapist."

O'Connell began his Bookshop tenure just six months after Gä Lombard started hers in the late '70s. "You bring in a seven-year-old who is interested in bugs," says O'Connell, "and Gä will have seven nonfiction titles on insects at her fingertips."

A significant percentage of Bookshop employees commit to a long-term career in bookselling. Among those who have worked twenty-plus years at the store are Stefanie Berntson, Judith Milton, Lori Fukuda, Kara Badger, Dave Friedman, Kelsey Ramage and George Balassone.

Berntson has been bringing her twin nine-year-old daughters into Bookshop's children's section since they were old enough to hold a book. As a child, she developed an abiding interest in illustration and thought she might be a children's book illustrator at one point. Among her most prized possessions are two notes from Dr. Seuss, handwritten in crayon. But as a book buyer and marketing manager at Bookshop for more than twenty years, Berntson brings a different idiosyncratic passion that is reflected in the store's inventory.

"I'm all about cookbooks," she says. "If I had a dream job, if I could do only one thing in this store, I would give it all up just to do cookbooks."

Books about food have mushroomed as a genre in the last decade – traditional cookbooks, ethnic cookbooks, diet/nutrition titles, science books about cooking, food memoirs, arguments for healthy eating or sustainable farming, travel books about food, Anthony Bourdain, Michael Pollan, Ruth Reichl. It has become a specialty at Bookshop because of the consuming passion that Berntson brings to the subject. She insists that cookbooks can and do reach into the realm of meaningful literature. "The kind of stuff that really moves me are the family stories, the immigrant stories, the personal stories that are behind these cookbooks," she says.

These kinds of booksellers are the indie bookstore's not-so-secret weapon. There is a love for books that is deeply shared by readers of all kinds. "I'd rather smell a book than a chocolate bar," says poet Patrice Vecchione. At the same time, it's also the kind of love that can get stuck in vague abstraction. Only when you bore down into genre and subgenre and sub-subgenre do you find layers of richness and variety of experience that mass culture can't bother with. Ask a bookseller at an indie bookstore about their particular obsession and buckle up for a wild ride.

For Bookshop Santa Cruz to have survived fifty years, it needed the loyalty of its customer base, the commitment of employees, the support of brethren indie booksellers and the faith of Santa Cruz's readers, writers and book lovers. It needed every bit of Neal's risk-taking moxie, every bit of Candy's day-to-day human touch, and every bit of Casey's cool-headed competence and commitment to tapping the collective wisdom of her staff.

"One of the things about the Coonertys," says O'Connell, "is they run a remarkably democratic company. They really have sought out the input of people who work here. It's not a cooperative. It's not a collective. Not everyone has the same amount of power or authority. But that office door is usually open. That's one of the things that has made this a richer store: They have hired capable people and they listen to them."

The post-Borders years at Bookshop were a period of aggressive thinking on how best to serve a marketplace that was changing in unpredictable ways. The store brought in the Espresso Book Machine, designed to print otherwise unavailable books while you wait, particularly self-published titles designed for small audiences. The machine itself didn't last long at Bookshop, but it established the basis for a strong partnership between Bookshop and local writers that continues with self-publishing services. Casey Protti and her staff also initiated and supported a number of programs to raise Bookshop's profile and serve the community, including its popular summer reading program for young people, an annual young writer's contest, an annual short-story contest, a photography contest featuring photos of people reading, partnerships with local schools to support a books blog for teens and hosting mixers to establish book groups. Bookshop also went out to where potential readers might be with its outdoor programs and its Books & Brews events at local brewpubs.

To survive, though, they also needed a lightning bolt or two from the cosmos, an intervention from a god with a weakness for O. Henry ironies. There's a better than even chance that Bookshop would not be around today without the unanticipated revenue created by the Bush Countdown Clock and the sudden implosion of the Borders empire. That means the shaggy Berkeley liberal, the embodiment and image of the Santa Cruz-style progressive, a man willing to risk alienating conservative customers and losing money by mocking Nixon and Gingrich and Limbaugh – that man has to live with the possibility that George W. Bush saved his business. And it also means that, if you buy the theory that Amazon and the e-commerce revolution it spawned was the ultimate cause of the death of Borders, then Bookshop Santa Cruz owes dues to the devil, or at least a begrudging thanks.

There is a cartoon I like that still hangs on a wall way in back at Bookshop Santa Cruz. Published in an alternative weekly newspaper sometime after the opening of Borders in Santa Cruz was announced, it shows a pigeon-toed Neal Coonerty, slingshot in hand, in the kind of outfit Russell Crowe might have worn in *Gladiator*, the box-office behemoth of that time. Behind him is a hairy giant, obviously slain, lying flat on his back. On the giant's loincloth is emblazoned "Super Crown Books." To Coonerty's right, we see another giant in sandals and toga, this one standing menacingly with his fist clinched ready to brawl. Neal's shoulders sag as he says, "Not again."

The David-and-Goliath mythos is a tempting fit, but Neal Coonerty will be the first to tell you there's no truth in it. He didn't bring down Super Crown and he didn't bring down Borders. Bookshop was saved from those two threats by larger commercial forces that had almost nothing to do with Bookshop's efforts at guerilla resistance. A more accurate cartoon might show Coonerty as one of those tiny, insect-feeding proto-mammals at the time of the dinosaurs with Borders and Super Crown as giant, shrieking tyrannosauri.

An Irishman born on St. Patrick's Day is never going to completely discount the role of luck. However, even if Super Crown and Borders were going to collapse anyway, Coonerty's pugnacious, defiant leadership remains the primary factor that allowed Bookshop to reach its fiftieth anniversary. His example had hundreds of ripple effects, within his community and without. It took both of his children, for example, to fill his shoes: son Ryan on the political path, daughter Casey at Bookshop. As a prominent figure in the American Booksellers Association, he became nationally recognized as the guy who fought the chains and also survived Mother Nature.

Just how large a role Neal Coonerty played in the surprising and unlikely rebound of independent bookstores in this country really, in the end, isn't the point. He fought the good fight, he did what he loved, he made a difference – and now he can enjoy watching his daughter carry on that fight at a time of much more optimism. There is a cautious sense among booksellers, writers and readers that the ravages of the big-box store and Amazon have done their worst, and that those indies who have survived might continue to do so, barring some new rapacious threat. In the past few years, feature stories bearing good news for the industry have sprouted like banana slugs after a rain (it's a Santa Cruz thing). New indie bookstores are opening and older ones are thriving, they say. Surviving stores have gotten smarter and more savvy, they say. Customers have seen the light about the power of their buying habits to keep stores alive, they say. Even the potentially bad news that Amazon might open brick-and-mortar stores across the country is a concession of sorts that the corner book merchant is still valued.

What happens when you survive for fifty years in the face of unpredictable changes is that you come out the other end with a reputation, which is not always sensed up close. Novelist Elizabeth McKenzie travels to bookstores around the world, drops in on events that bring together writers, publishers and retailers. "Bookshop has upheld a standard for so many years of what it means to be an independent bookstore," she says. "And it has had so many dramatic turning points in its history. You go to other places and tell them you're from Santa Cruz and there's always this 'Ooooh, Bookshop Santa Cruz.' The Coonertys are kind of legendary. It makes you proud to be from Santa Cruz."

Epilogue

As a lifelong reader, I have until recently paid scant attention to the role that books have played in my own life. I grew up in a house where the bleatings of television filled one room or another from morning to midnight. The sad truth is that I spent much more time with, and was more deeply influenced by, Hawkeye Pierce and Fred Sanford than my own grandparents. I've drunk deep from popular music and movies all my life, and I've taken to the Internet Age like a sea turtle to salt water. But I have always found a way to carve out minutes and hours with books, on a Saturday morning, at night when everything is quiet, at lunch during the work week. It is not a discipline, like eating root vegetables, or jogging (unless you count *Finnegan's Wake* or *Infinite Jest*). It's a joy. Books are more than a distraction or a form of entertainment. They are points of reference, moral reassurances, blocks from which to build an identity. They are also wings, wheels, jet engines, whatever metaphor for purposeful motion you want to use. Books played a critical part in the most consequential decision of my life, to move to California.

It's 1984 and two young guys with freshly minted bachelor's

degrees and an apparent allergy to barbershops make a plan to travel across the United States, east to west, on what they fervently hope is a one-way trip to California. They have a 1979 Datsun 210 Hatchback. This is not a vacation; it's a move. So they must bring with them everything they'll need to start a new life. There is no roof rack, and no trailer. How much room do they have in the car for books? Not nearly enough.

Did I sacrifice something precious or essential to make room for those books? Did I take a moment to bid a tearful farewell to all my record albums before handing them off to my ungrateful kid brother? I can't say for sure. I just know we stocked up to be ready to make the most of the opportunities all those hours in the car would afford for the passenger to read aloud to the driver, which was exactly what we did.

Remember, this was a time when the calendar year shared its name with the title of one of the most resonant books of the twentieth century (though Orwell didn't make the cut in our collection). Ronald Reagan was running his "Morning in America" re-election campaign. The reigning Miss America popped up naked in the pages of *Penthouse* (that was one "book" we purchased en route) and the stage was set for the summer Olympics in Los Angeles, where the absence of the boycotting Soviet Union meant the U.S. of A. was gearing up for a pageant of breast-beating triumphalism. To us, a couple of brainy, weed-addled suburban boys with a rebellious streak more aspirational than actual, it all had to mean something. One thing we did know was that driving across Reagan's America to attend the L.A. Olympics sure sounded like a Hunter S. Thompson assignment, and that was exactly the pose we struck as we pulled out of Jay's driveway one day in Raleigh, North Carolina.

Of course, HST would have weighed down the Datsun with sheets of blotter acid, a couple of bottles of mezcal and "a pint of raw ether and two dozen amyls," as he hilariously chronicled in *Fear and Loathing in Las Vegas*. We were tame little hamsters compared to that. Instead, we packed a little bit of grass and a few Hunter Thompson books – *Fear and Loathing*, of course, as well as its sequel *Fear and Loathing on the Campaign Trail '72*, *Hell's Angels* and *The Curse of Lono*, which was, at the time, relatively new. There were others – Woody Allen's *Without Feathers*, a couple of those early Tom Wolfe books with the impossibly long titles, Tom Robbins' *Still Life with Woodpecker*, Richard Brautigan's *In Watermelon Sugar*, and Kerouac's *On the Road* (duh). Truth be told, we didn't indulge too much in the Kerouac. It existed alongside a few other titles that served more as holy relics of our trip than books to read aloud: Steinbeck's *The Grapes of Wrath*, Twain's *Innocents Abroad*, Whitman's *Leaves of Grass* (the only one of those books that I still own). Sure, we had our meticulously curated box of cassette tapes; I still think of the impossibly open vistas of the Great Plains whenever I hear Pat Metheny. But mostly, we read until our voices grew hoarse, silly absurdist prose that mocked the very idea of deeper meaning. Today, I might look at that box of books as so much performative, juvenile puffery, but at the time, it seemed the most appropriate way to weave through the Reagan-Bush signs that dotted the American interior was to read Tom Robbins.

Fear and Loathing was our holy writ. We rationed it, like a backpacker might ration a chocolate bar. We took our sweet time that summer, ambling about like a marble on a hardwood floor, traveling across the country in a route that resembled the line on an EKG, trending west in a giant north-south wave. But we had always planned to end up in Vegas and enter California via Barstow, just as HST did. (It didn't happen that way; we instead found ourselves much farther north and came in via I-80 through the High Sierra.)

Today, California often feels to me like just another place. A bored kid in Ohio might be as likely to bolt for Brooklyn or Austin or Portland or any place with a more favorable hipster-to-hayseed ratio than their own hometown. Back in the late '80s, though, there was still some trace amount of heady, purely American-style romance attached to packing it all up and heading to the Left Coast, even if talk of California as paradise was on the verge of evaporating away forever. California culture might have been morphing into some kind of Black Flag, Dead Kennedys vision of dashed promise, but my friend and I were still humming "Peaceful Easy Feeling" on our sojourn across America. My move west was only a generation removed from the nightmare of the Charles Manson murders, which became to the rest of the country emblematic of something hellish brewing out there in the land of hot tubs and surfboards. Jim Morrison growling "The West is the best/ Get here and we'll do the rest" was playing on these dark visions long before even the Manson murders. Throughout the 1970s, for much of the rest of the country, California was a stage on which was playing the unraveling of their good, Christian nation.

Those fine conservative people made no distinction between the murderous Manson and the liberating spirit of, say, Harvey Milk. To them, it was different faces of the same cult of hedonistic individualism. There was a madness in those warm, scented breezes, which turned bright attractive young people into half-naked, dope-smoking zombies who would besmirch their family name for laughs and sacrifice their very identity to any number of messianic, charismatic nut jobs. If it could happen to Patricia Hearst, as close to royalty as you could find in California, it could happen to any other Patricia in Wisconsin, South Carolina or Oklahoma. California was the stranger in the van luring the cute little boys and girls in the neighborhood with candy and soothing promises. And in the kitchens and living rooms of the other America, those news stories about Manson and Hearst and Jim Jones were all parts of the same grand narrative. This was a time when *Reader's Digest* ran stories of heroic fathers tracking down their wayward daughters in some rural Northern California commune. With the help of professionals in these matters, strong, broad-shouldered Dad would drag his beautiful Patricia to a roadside motel, kicking and screaming if necessary, and break the malignant spell the counterculture had on her. Right beside this harrowing testimonial, there it would be, a photo of Dad with his beaming adult daughter, now a nursing student at the local community college in Iowa, Tennessee or New Hampshire.

This is what California looked like on the outside, and this is why kids' doing what just about every generation of American got to do before them, packing up and following the setting sun, was seen as something akin to tragedy, like losing a child to drug abuse. By the mid-'80s, the Beach Boys' Brian Wilson, a major player in creating the overripe vision of California romanticism, was sinking into mental illness. His brother Dennis, the only Beach Boy who actually surfed, and who himself got tied up with Charlie Manson, had drowned while drunk only a few months before my trip west. The AIDS epidemic was destroying San Francisco's bathhouse culture, and those who preferred the comfort of moral smugness over empathy and humanity whispered among themselves about retribution. This is why, in 1984, in North Carolina, you didn't go around telling your mother's country-club friends that you were moving to California with no job, no connections and no plan. So I kept quiet, feeding my determination to go through with it by reading the stories of those who had traveled that path already. I read a bit of the history stuff, the Donner Party story, a bit of the primary source memoirs of the pioneers on the Oregon Trail. I started *Grapes of Wrath*. But I also read those pulpy novels that they used to sell in the supermarkets, the kind with the raised lettering and firm-jawed white people on the cover, the kind about wagon trails and Western settlement by people like James Michener and Dana Fuller Ross.

The part that thrilled me most in those novels, a moment that I'm sure happened thousands and thousands of times during the nineteenth century in ways too moving and poignant for even pulp novels to approximate, was that moment in Pennsylvania or Virginia or Alabama when the pioneer, his wagon all packed with provisions, grabbed his weeping mother by the shoulders and told her simply but clearly a variation of this: "Goodbye. You will not see me again in this life. We'll reunite one day in the sweet hereafter." That's what going to California used to cost: everything.

The impulse to move west is a pull, but it's a push too. You need to have a tailwind, something tangible to leave behind to give your hope a distinct shape because long before young people figure out what they want, they learn what they don't want. Ultimately, it was upon books that I built my justification for leaving my family and starting over, not only the stories and messages contained in those books, but what they represented in the context of my own life. Taken as a text, I've always thought *On the Road* was a tedious, sloppy novel. But the spirit of that book – we had a weathered paperback from the edition with the setting sun on its cover – its symbolic aura as the magic key to the liberation from one's upbringing, well, to me it was palpable. I could almost feel it radiating up from behind the passenger seat of the Datsun.

For me, the trip to California did indeed turn out to be one way. I raised a family, cultivated a career and made a home on the Pacific Coast. If my parents, all those years ago, questioned how the bookish kid who never seemed to leave the house could possibly catapult to the other side of the country and never come back, their failure of vision was the same that many people make. Seen from the outside, the act of reading a book looks like a stationary, sedentary act. In fact, it's the opposite: Writers and avid readers alike are setting off on journeys, often transformative journeys.

Though I didn't know it at the time, that road that my buddy and

I first set out on led ultimately to Bookshop Santa Cruz. In telling the remarkable story of the Coonerty family and their importance to a community and beyond, I've been privileged to inhabit a unique history that not only reflects many of the larger currents of American life in macrocosm, but also contains many of the great elements of storytelling that we turn to books for in the first place.

As a newspaper arts columnist, I've celebrated creative people and their works for many years. It's the kind of job that fosters and reinforces the belief that at some deep, unspoken level, nurturing the arts matters, that support and encouragement and understanding could help put a good project or visionary idea over the top and we'd all be the better for it. Literary communities aren't built like greenhouses from blueprints. They emerge and evolve in favorable conditions like wildflower meadows or palm groves in the desert.

Writers, despite compelling evidence to the contrary, are social beings after all. Writing as it's happening often feels like shouting into the abyss, talking to the wall or whispering in the ear of a statue. For too many writers, publishing feels like that too. As much as they need ample time to spelunk into the corners and recesses of their imaginations, writers also need a toehold in the consensus reality we call the real world. Against that backdrop, a bookstore as robust and energetic as Bookshop Santa Cruz is much more than a building in which to buy books. For writers and readers alike, it's like a campfire in the night, drawing you in for a bit of emotional and artistic sustenance before you retreat again to your pup tent to engage with your book. Without that beacon, especially in an era of such rapid and confusing technological change, it looks awfully dark outside.

A world that once produced Tolstoy now communicates by tweets at one hundred forty characters at a time. We've evolved from the Lincoln-Douglas debates to Donald Trump playing around with hashtags. For giant swaths of the populace, reading books is as foreign an act as eating grasshoppers. Despite the

Harry Potter revolution of the late 1990s, we can't quite shake the suspicion that younger generations are not as bonded to reading books as an essential part of everyday life. I once gave as a college graduation gift to a young person I know a copy of David Foster Wallace's short but magnificent book-length essay *This Is Water,* adapted from his famous 2005 commencement speech. Months later, when I found out that the book was unread and left behind, it bothered me more than it should have. It is indicative of nothing, I know. I am as guilty as anyone of not reading books foisted upon me by others (it's in my job description as a journalist). Still, it was a helpful reminder that the connection between one reader and another through the conduit of a particular book is more rare than we suppose and we should treasure it when it happens.

Book lovers know that reading is essential like they know their blood is red. You don't have to tell them that reading – whether it's literature, journalism, science or poetry – is the engine of cultural and economic progress. The brilliant British writer Neil Gaiman tells the story of traveling to China to participate in the first government-approved science-fiction convention there. A puzzled Gaiman asked a top official why the Chinese were suddenly allowing something they had previously banned. Turns out, a Chinese delegation was sent to Silicon Valley to find out how companies like Google and Apple were able to keep innovating. Did they have a secret? Many of the visionaries the delegation spoke to had something in common: They had all read science fiction as kids. The Chinese concluded that the power of books to generate ideas and innovation had to be tapped, at least carefully.

People who love books do so with a unique brand of devotion. The love of books may not be "greater" (whatever that means) than the love of a wedding dress, or a sports car, or perhaps the world's only bobblehead collection that contains Thomas Jefferson *and* Daisy Duke (maybe I'm revealing too much here). But book love is certainly of a different character. Dave Eggers collects different editions of Saul Bellow's *Herzog*. Goodreads founder Otis Chandler still carries around a copy of Frank Herbert's *Dune* that belonged to his father. The late novelist and book critic Alan Cheuse (also a Santa Cruzan) claimed that seeing a first edition of James Joyce's *Ulysses* was as close to a religious experience as he ever got. Ask anyone interesting (writer or otherwise) and you'll hear a similar story.

Love of books is something both ephemeral and tactile. It colors people's relationships, how they view the world. It even, in some of the more hardcore cases, constitutes a notion of heaven. Maybe the single most enduring episode of *The Twilight Zone* was from the show's first season, featuring Burgess Meredith as a bookworm banker who can never find the time to do the one thing he wants to do most in the world, read. When a nuclear explosion makes him the only survivor in a post-apocalyptic world (he was hiding in the bank's vault reading when the Bomb hit), he is saved from despair by the thundering insight that he is now free to read all he wants when he wants. Elated, he picks up the first book in the ruins of a public library and promptly stumbles, causing his eyeglasses to fall off and shatter. End of reading idyll. OK, so the irony is not going to win any awards for subtlety, but for anyone who loves books, it's a story that makes the blood go cold.

People who love books take certain things for granted: that reading is fundamental to education, and education is fundamental to a "good life," in the Aristotelian sense of the term; that reading is the fuel of the human imagination; that it breeds empathy and compassion; that it is the closest thing to a time machine and a means to immortality that we are ever likely to have. Sure, we think we've won the argument that reading has great societal value that must be supported. But we live in an age where old assumptions are being discarded, a time of revisiting discussions we thought we had long since moved past. In a culture that can't agree on what a fact is, values can never be completely secured. It's no longer outlandish to think that an opportunistic demagogue could make the pitch that literacy is for prissy elites, that anyone with their nose in a book is a leech on a society built by those who do "real" work, that telling stories and creating metaphors are mere entertainment, and for that we have sports and reality TV.

Every day we live with the real risk of having more people slide away from the world of books and the deeper perspective that books bring, which means that every day we who care about books have to fight for their role in our national life. The real heroes in that fight are those on the front lines, Neal Coonerty and Casey Coonerty Protti and every bookseller at Bookshop Santa Cruz and at every independent bookstore. I hope their story will inspire you to show your support for your local independent and encourage others to do the same, order a book there rather than online, but above all, let the people who devote their lives to these independents know that they matter to you, let them know that they are a meaningful part of your life as a reader.

ACKNOWLEDGEMENTS

It's been an amazing privilege for me to play a small role in the celebration of the fifty-year anniversary of one of America's grandest independent bookstores by telling its story. My deepest gratitude goes to my friend and publisher Steve Kettmann of Wellstone Books who initiated this project, placed it confidently in my hands and exercised a strong guiding voice throughout. It was a nourishing and illuminating collaboration. Thanks, Steve. Big thanks to my editor Pete Danko, who worked hard to help me clarify my ideas and streamline the story.

I'm also indebted to all those who shared their perspectives on Bookshop Santa Cruz, including the store's very first employee (and my first interview) Jon Scoville, Lee Quarnstrom, Steve Jensen, Lisa Jensen, Ralph Abraham, Sharon Lau, Patrice Vecchione, Richard Lange, Maryse Meijer, Jonathan Franzen, Laurie R. King, Richard Howorth, Gwen Marcum, Geoffrey Dunn, Jeanne Wakatsuki Houston, Richard Wilson, David Zeltser, Elizabeth McKenzie, Stefanie Berntson, Phyllis Cohen, Ceil Cirillo and Patrick O'Connell. Thanks also to my beautiful wife Tina for her encouragement and love (and patience).

A deep bow too goes to Third District Santa Cruz County Supervisor Ryan Coonerty and Bookshop Santa Cruz owner/operator Casey Coonerty Protti, the brother/sister duo who have both been so deeply entwined with Bookshop that they may as well have been born in the store. (My guess is that Ryan would have come into the world in the humor section in the shadow of the Art Buchwald books, and Casey would have announced her presence in between the poetry and mystery sections.)

Finally, it's been a great honor for me to share time and stories with the hero of this book, the wise, warm and just a little bit weird Mr. Neal Coonerty, the shaggy Berkeley grad who talked his way into landing a bookstore at twenty-seven and then followed every crazy gut instinct to keep it going. It shouldn't have worked, but somehow it did. You sir are, as the kids say these days, a total bad ass.

PICTURED LEFT TO RIGHT:
Ryan Coonerty, Neal Coonerty and Casey Coonerty Protti

SUPPORT YOUR LOCAL INDEPENDENT:
About the Series

Wallace Baine brings alive in these pages an unforgettable scene:
An earthquake-ravaged bookstore, roof in danger of caving in at
any moment, and the brave people who ventured inside to save
the books: First burly, bearded Bookshop Santa Cruz owner Neal
Coonerty, a larger-than-life personality, then a legion of loyal readers
from the community who showed up to sign a waiver saying they
understood they were risking their lives to save books. Now, nearly
thirty years later, Bookshop Santa Cruz is a more vibrant institution
than ever, reaching out to the community under the forward-think-
ing leadership of Casey Coonerty Protti, Neal's daughter, offering
a regular lineup of great author events and never missing a chance
to have fun with their love of books. A bookstore like Bookshop
both captures and generates a magic that rubs off on everyone who
sets foot inside, and we're proud to kick off our Wellstone Books'
"Support Your Local Independent" series with this volume. Only a
few years ago, doom and gloom infiltrated all talk of the future of
books, but there's room now to exhale and take pleasure in all that
books offer devoted readers. We're on the lookout for established
writers looking to author a love letter to their favorite independent bookstore. Too often, we're too busy or distracted to celebrate
cultural heroes, people who really do make a difference, people like
the Coonerty family and so many others who have made Bookshop
Santa Cruz what it is today. If you have a suggestion for another
independent to celebrate, email Wellstone Books Publisher Steve
Kettmann directly at steve@wellstoneredwoods.org

About Wellstone Books

Wellstone Books is the publishing arm of the Wellstone Center in the Redwoods – **www.wellstoneredwoods.org** – a small writers' retreat center in Northern California that offers writing residencies, fellowships and three-month resident internships for aspiring writers, and holds regular Author Talk events with writers like novelists Matt Gallagher and Viet Thanh Nguyen. Wellstone Books focuses on California fiction and personal writing that is not afraid to inspire. We do not accept unsolicited manuscripts, but are always looking for writers who are familiar with our publishing philosophy and want to work with us to develop future projects. Interested writers, or journalists in search of review copies or author availability, write to:

books@wellstoneredwoods.org

Also Available From Wellstone Books

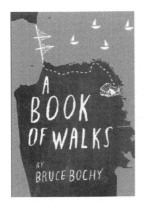

A Book of Walks
By Bruce Bochy

The manager of the San Francisco Giants, having taken his team to World Series victories in 2010, 2012 and 2014, is known nationally for his rare knack for staying on an even keel even in the midst of some very stressful situations. How does he do it? One thing he's always tried to do is get in regular long walks, which help him clear his head and get over the disappointments of the day. This pocket-sized volume, dubbed "an endearing little book" by the *New York Times*, takes us with Bochy on eight talks around the country, each its own chapter (complete with map of his route). Come along for the ride on walks through Central Park in New York, along Lake Michigan in Chicago and across San Francisco to the Golden Gate Bridge. How does Bochy keep a cool head, the Toronto *Globe and Mail* asked?

"In the tradition of thinkers like Rousseau, Kant and Thoreau, Bochy, sixty, swears by long strolls and vigorous walks – 'the freedom to be alone with my thoughts for a while' – which he makes time for wherever he is," Nathalie Atkinson writes.

A Book of Walks, a Northern California bestseller, makes a memorable gift for any baseball fan – or fan of walks.

Night Running: A Book of Essays About Breaking Through

This daring volume combines the best of writing on running with the appeal of the best literary writing, essays that take in the sights and sounds and smells of real life, of real risk, of real pain and of real elation. Emphasizing female voices, this collection of eleven personal essays set in different countries around the world offers a deep but accessible look at the power of running in our lives to make us feel more and to see ourselves in a new light.

From acclaimed novelist Emily Mitchell and Portland writers Anne Milligan and Pete Danko and authors Vanessa Runs and Steve Kettmann to Bonnie Ford, T.J. Quinn and Joy Russo-Schoenfield of ESPN, a diverse lineup of writers captures a variety of perspectives on running at night. These are stories that can inspire people of all ages and backgrounds to take on a thrilling new challenge. The contributors all have distinct tales to tell, but each brings a freshness and depth to their experiences that make *Night Running* a necessary part of every runner's library - and a valuable addition to the reading lists of all thoughtful readers. We're putting together a Night Running 2 collection; writers interested in contributing should email us at info@wellstoneredwoods.org for guidelines.

"A book for anyone who has used solitude and exertion to explore a new crevice of their own mind. Fear, exhilaration, anger, accomplishment, despair, euphoria – every one of these emotions is distilled in *Night Running*."
— David Epstein, *The Sports Gene*

"A fascinating and eclectic collection! In Night Running, eleven essayists express, with bracing honesty, how a simple act of will—running in the dark—can free body and mind from fear, and restore the spirit."
— Novelist Mary Volmer, author of *Crown of Dust* and *Reliance, Illinois*

"*Night Running* captures in a myriad of ways the essence of running: solitude, self-discovery and the exhilaration of a momentary escape from the banal."
— Sandy Alderson, general manager, New York Mets, 2:53 marathoner